Story Deep

Story Deep

How to Find Hidden Treasures of Meaning

As You Study Bible Stories

Randal Gilmore

Cover Design by Dori Durbin
ISBN: 978-1-7325000-6-8
Copyright © 2022 Randal L. Gilmore
All Rights Reserved
EXALT Publications, Fishers, IN

What Others Are Saying...

Story Deep is extremely helpful to me as a pastor and as someone who is regularly preaching and teaching. Even if you're not a pastor, if you're reading through the Scripture devotionally, this will help you...I highly recommend it for those in Christian ministry or for the Christian who just wants to be encouraged in the truth of God's Word.

Pastor Adam Breiner, Gilbertsville, PA

Read Story Deep to expand your understanding of the stories within the Bible. In addition, you'll receive a fresh new way of sharing your faith.

Peg Clayton, M.A., Missionary and ESL Curriculum Specialist

Dr. Gilmore's devotion to understanding the role of storying has greatly impacted my love for Bible narrative. I have been teaching the Book of Acts in Bible colleges in Brazil and the United States for nearly three decades. However, in more recent years, my interaction with him has kindled a new thirst for the beauty of the story itself, rather than the sophistication of clever outlines and abstract summaries. This book is a guide to that end, and I commend it to anyone desiring to mine the riches of the Bible's incomparable story.

Dr. Mark Lounsbrough, Missions Professor

So good! Altering how I think through the Bible stories I'm reading to the kids!

Kara, Mother of Four

Story Deep provides an eye-opening look at how modern-day sermon outlines and alliteration can sometimes fall short in communicating the full story of who Jesus is and what he has done. Dr. Gilmore's practical approach to understanding how to tell a Biblical story, along with the examples provided in this book, will enable the reader to apply these concepts to other passages of Scripture in order to enhance audience understanding of the complete story the whole Bible is telling of the salvation God offers each of us.

Lee Schultz, Instructional Systems Specialist

The Bible tells the world's greatest story, and Story Deep provides a way of understanding stories. Anyone preaching or teaching Biblical stories must understand how a story works both within itself and within the overarching storyline, and this book provides understanding and methods to help. I look forward to using Story Deep methods personally and in ministry.

Andrew Gonnerman, Missionary to Japan

This book will make a difference in how listeners of your teaching and preaching of God's Word will respond. The expository preaching of one word, one sentence, one verse, one chapter and one book of the Bible is contained in the whole, entire, 'deep' story of the Word of God! Read it. It will make a difference!

Pastor Jim Kester, Tucson, AZ

After reading Story Deep I am really excited to apply the Story Deep process to Bible stories I have read many times. I feel like a new door has opened for me to gain insight into God's word and go deeper into the inexhaustible depths of scripture!

Charles Harting, Fishers, IN

My Daily Promise

In pursuit of God's kingdom, and by his will and grace, and according to the righteous plans he brings to me, I will use the science of story...

- To better tell who Jesus is, and to foster appreciative love for him

- To connect the dots of Jesus' story in Scripture, and to communicate the connections

- To practice a Jesus-centered worldview

- And to prepare myself and others for Jesus' return

—Randal Gilmore

Table of Contents

Acres of Diamonds

Many years ago, I heard the phrase "acres of diamonds" in a story by Earl Nightingale. Nightingale shares the tale of a poor African farmer who sells his land and sets out in search of diamonds, hoping to find a productive mine and become rich. But the farmer fails and dies empty-handed. Meanwhile, things pan out differently for the man who purchased the farmer's land. He goes for a walk one day and discovers a large precious stone in a stream. It was a diamond of incalculable value. The man sloshed around in the streambed and found others like it. In time, his newly acquired property became one of the world's richest diamond mines.

Nightingale's tale is the perfect metaphor for explaining why I've written Story Deep. The stories we find in Scripture are like the acres of diamonds. Imagine we are the poor farmer, unaware of the riches they hold. But there they are, right in front of us, diamonds of all sizes, this one hiding in a streambed, another nearby. Still others lie buried so deep that only a certain type of effort will find them. Or imagine knowing the diamonds are there, but not having the right equipment for retrieving them.

That brings us to Story Deep. I've written Story Deep with four objectives in mind. First, to remind us all that Bible stories contain a mother lode of hidden treasures of meaning. Second, to identify the right equipment for mining these treasures. Third, to show you how to use the equipment. And fourth, to share the exhilaration of discovery.

My first aha-moment

I'll never forget my first aha-moment in Scripture soon after I turned 13. One afternoon, I pedaled my red Schwinn bike five miles from my house to a special place I found beneath a bridge over Sugar Creek. I sat in the shade under a tall sycamore, pulled out a pocket-size New Testament, and opened it to Romans 8:38-39. I don't know why my eyes landed there; but, as I read, the words leaped off the page into my heart. I was deeply moved by the promise of nothing ever separating me from the love of God in Christ Jesus; nothing at all, "neither death nor life, nor angels nor rulers, nor things present nor things to come, nor powers, nor height nor depth, nor anything else in creation." I repeated these words over and over, etching them on the pages of my heart. To this day, I can still recall both verses and feel the same joyful exhilaration.

When I say *joyful exhilaration*, I'm referring to a response that comes from deep within a person's heart, a response much like what the two disciples in Luke 24 experienced on their way to Emmaus. Their hearts "burned within them" as they listened to Jesus interpret his story in all the Scriptures, "beginning with Moses and all the Prophets."

My prayer is that Story Deep will convince you of the potential for your own exhilarating peak experiences with the Lord through the study of Bible stories. I desire for you to know the lively joy of a burning heart, not just from the exposition of discourse passages like Romans 8:38-39, but also of their counterparts in story.

False beliefs and old habits

Your reading this book speaks volumes of your interest in the study of God's Word. You could be a pastor or someone preparing for vocational ministry. You could be a lay Bible teacher, youth leader, or member of a small group. Whichever you are, you're the type of person who loves God's Word and desires to maximize its impact in your life.

I share this same love and desire. But it's possible I also share experiences that can lead to false beliefs about studying Bible stories as *story*. These false beliefs include: *If I refer to Bible stories as story, people might not believe they're true. Or they'll stop thinking of me as a serious Bible teacher. They'll see me instead as a storyteller or entertainer. Or that I'm trying to be trendy.*

These are what I believed. Then I learned a very narrow definition of the word *story*, a definition that changed my mind, and that I'll share in the next chapter. I also learned the ties between *story* and neuroscience, and *story's* potential for spreading truth in ways that stick. One researcher goes so far as to say: "Story is the interstate highway into the mind."

Other false beliefs were just as controlling: *Bible stories are for children. Adults need word studies and outlines—the more clever, more alliterated, and more parallel their construction, the better. Throw in a few illustrations, better still. Otherwise, adults will never learn doctrine.*

Around the same time, I remember reading from a commentary on 1 Corinthians 11. I know that Paul's letter to the Corinthians is not a story. The commentator knew it too. His analysis reflected it. He approached the text with impeccable logic, pontificating over inferences he saw there. But not just first-level inferences; he wrote on and on about second- and third-level inferences—inferences of inferences of inferences. In short order, the text itself seemed as distant as a far-off planet. I remember thinking, *There's no way the Corinthians understood Paul's letter like this!*

Then I realized I had been using a similar approach in my teaching, even when my texts were Bible stories. I would focus on their theological inferences with logical outlines and word studies. But I seldom bothered with discerning or telling the stories themselves as *stories*. I didn't even know how.

So I dived into the literature. Books, journal articles, and websites came first. I took online courses, watched YouTube videos, and listened to podcasts. I wanted to develop an expertise in *story* that I could both use and share. My focus wasn't on individual Bible stories alone. It was also on *the overarching story told in Scripture about Jesus.*

An Overview

In Story Deep, I offer an overview of the many things I've learned about studying biblical narrative. I emphasize the word *overview*. This won't be an exhaustive manual. I could never pack everything about story hermeneutics into just one book. Still, there is a lot here, enough to get you started, and then to grow, your desire for more.

Chapter 1 identifies the first step in a story deep process: *Read the Story*. In this chapter, I also provide the definition of *story* that I referred to earlier, as well as a list of story elements to look for as we study. Chapter 2 builds on this list, identifying 21 additional story terms to be aware of.

Chapter 3 covers the next step: *Ask Story Questions*. Story questions rise from attempts to make sense of what happens in a story. Asking them early in the study process rebuffs the habit of starting instead with searches for theological propositions.

Chapters 4 and 5 reveal why logical outlines are the wrong tool for mining diamonds hidden in Bible stories. In these chapters, I detail how logical outlining of Bible stories interferes with principles of inductive Bible study.

Chapters 6 and 7 advocate tying individual Bible stories to the larger story about Jesus in the rest of Scripture, and to the rest of an author's work, whether in the same book or not.

Chapters 8-10 detail three additional steps in a story deep process: *Create a Step-Outline*; *Treat the Step Outline*; and *Treat the Story's Structure*. The tools in these chapters are the most sophisticated in the story deep tool shed. For many, this will be the first time they've heard of these tools, much less used them. And yet these are the tools that prove most helpful in answering story questions, especially when the answers aren't otherwise apparent. So these chapters slow down to show you how to use each tool.

Chapters 11-13 represent the final steps of a story deep process: *Answer Story Questions*; *Apply the Story*; and *Teach the Story*.

Not a linear process

The specific activities tied to each chapter won't restrict you to a linear study process. The activities loop and repeat. Noted authors Traina and Bauer label this type of movement in inductive study as a *spiral*. The back and forth will help you guard against invalid interpretations. I'll write more later about the helpful work of Traina and Bauer. For now, I want to call your attention to two other comments they make on inductive Bible study. The first concerns what they call *the inductive spirit*. This they define as the "attitude" that goes before the inductive process. Traina and Bauer further explain:

"The test of the inductive spirit is whether one's approach is characterized by radical openness to any conclusion required by the biblical evidence. This attitude is the inner dimension of the inductive approach, while any specific process that might be considered inductive is its outer expression and implementation."

Bauer, David R.; Traina, Robert A.. Inductive Bible Study (p. 18). Baker Publishing Group. Kindle Edition.

Traina and Bauer also emphasize that their method is not the only one that qualifies as inductive. Nor must students of the Word labor through every bit of their process to count their work as inductive:

"The inductive process is whatever is most effective and efficient in determining the meaning of the text and thus effectuating or implementing an inductive attitude."

Bauer, David R.; Traina, Robert A.. Inductive Bible Study (p. 20). Baker Publishing Group. Kindle Edition.

The Story Deep method also aims for "a radical openness to any conclusion required by biblical evidence," while acknowledging the possibility of other types of inductive approaches.

Stick with it

Some may feel overwhelmed by the sheer volume of things to consider when studying Bible stories as *story*. They'll find it tempting to return to their former methods of systematizing stories for their theological inferences. I often share that learning to treat Bible stories as *stories* can be like trying to learn a new way to tie shoes. Most of us learned how to tie shoes at very young ages. Through repetition over the years, we develop muscle memory and no longer have to think about what we're doing. But if we tried to learn a new way to tie shoes, we'd have to concentrate. Otherwise, we'd be all thumbs. But here's the kicker: *the frustration that comes with acquiring new muscle memory is enough to make most of us give up and return to what's familiar.* Applying this analogy to learning the story deep process, I want to encourage you to stick with it and don't give up. Think of the individual parts of the process as the specialized mining equipment you need for digging deep and uncovering diamonds. Keep in mind also, even if you don't use every tool in every one of your studies, the parts you do use will grow your skills as a faithful expositor of Bible stories.

Disciples on the road to Emmaus and How to Read this Book

I've selected the story of the two disciples on the road to Emmaus in Luke 24 to show you how to use a story deep method. I'm sharing this now because you may prefer to begin reading this book with Chapters 12 and 13, the chapters that summarize the results of the story deep process. Starting there will provide context for my explanations in earlier chapters. Appendix A offers a quick overview of the story deep process and may also provide a helpful starting point for some. Appendix B features a retelling of the Emmaus story based on Luke's not naming the second disciple. I wrote this retelling a few months prior to writing this book, as I was pondering how to apply the story's central meaning in a creative way. Appendix C summarizes the case for a story-first approach to help us overcome the dissonance the world stirs up in our lives.

Finally, if it's not already clear, you'll soon be able to tell the story of the Emmaus disciples has become one of my all-time favorites. It features the possibility of exhilarating peak experiences with Jesus and his Word, tied to the study of Bible stories as *story*. I can't wait to show you.

Chapter 1

Read the Story

The map is not the territory. I heard this famous saying for the first time in graduate school at Western Michigan University. Its meaning is plain. Even the most detailed map can't take the place of the actual territory it represents.

The same principle applies to the study of Bible narratives. No matter how insightful the fruit of our study will be, the story itself remains primary. Our analysis is not the story. Therefore, the first step in the *story deep* method is *Read the story*.

Luke 24:13-53:

> [13] That very day two of them were going to a village named Emmaus, about seven miles from Jerusalem, [14] and they were talking with each other about all these things that had happened. [15] While they were talking and discussing together, Jesus himself drew near and went with them. [16] But their eyes were kept from recognizing him. [17] And he said to them, "What is this conversation that you are holding with each other as you walk?" And they stood still, looking sad. [18] Then one of them, named Cleopas, answered him, "Are you the only visitor to Jerusalem who does not know the things that

have happened there in these days?" ¹⁹ And he said to them, "What things?" And they said to him, "Concerning Jesus of Nazareth, a man who was a prophet mighty in deed and word before God and all the people, ²⁰ and how our chief priests and rulers delivered him up to be condemned to death, and crucified him. ²¹ But we had hoped that he was the one to redeem Israel. Yes, and besides all this, it is now the third day since these things happened. ²² Moreover, some women of our company amazed us. They were at the tomb early in the morning, ²³ and when they did not find his body, they came back saying that they had even seen a vision of angels, who said that he was alive. ²⁴ Some of those who were with us went to the tomb and found it just as the women had said, but him they did not see." ²⁵ And he said to them, "O foolish ones, and slow of heart to believe all that the prophets have spoken! ²⁶ Was it not necessary that the Christ should suffer these things and enter into his glory?" ²⁷ And beginning with Moses and all the Prophets, he interpreted to them in all the Scriptures the things concerning himself. ²⁸ So they drew near to the village to which they were going. He acted as if he were going farther, ²⁹ but they urged him strongly, saying, "Stay with us, for it is toward evening and the day is now far spent." So he went in to stay with them. ³⁰ When he was at table with them, he took the bread and blessed and broke it and gave it to them. ³¹ And their eyes were opened, and they recognized him. And he vanished from their sight. ³² They said to each other, "Did not our hearts burn within us while he talked to us on the road, while he opened to us the Scriptures?" ³³ And they rose that same hour and returned to Jerusalem. And they found the eleven and those who were with them gathered together, ³⁴ saying, "The Lord has risen indeed, and has appeared to Simon!" ³⁵ Then they told what had happened on the road, and how he was known to them in the breaking of the bread. ³⁶ As they were talking about these things, Jesus himself stood among them, and said to them, "Peace to you!" ³⁷ But they were startled and frightened and thought they saw a spirit. [38] And he said to them, "Why are you troubled, and why do doubts arise in your hearts? [39] See my hands and my feet, that it is I myself. Touch me, and see. For a spirit does not have flesh and bones as you see that I have." [40] And when he had said this, he showed them his hands and his feet. [41] And while they still disbelieved for joy and were marveling, he said to them, "Have you anything here to eat?" [42] They gave him a piece of broiled fish, [43] and he took it and ate before them. [44] Then he said to them, "These are my words that I spoke to you while I was still with you, that everything written about me in the Law of Moses and the Prophets and the Psalms must be fulfilled." [45] Then he opened their minds to understand the Scriptures, [46] and said to them, "Thus it is written, that the Christ should suffer and on the third day rise from the dead, [47] and that repentance and forgiveness of sins should be proclaimed in his name to all nations, beginning from Jerusalem. [48] You are witnesses of these things. [49] And behold, I am sending the promise of my Father upon you. But stay in the city until you are clothed with power from on high." [50] Then he led them out as far as Bethany, and lifting up his hands he blessed them. [51] While he blessed them, he parted from them and was carried up into heaven. [52] And they worshiped him and returned to Jerusalem with great joy, [53] and were continually in the temple blessing God.

Read the story again and again to become familiar with it. Familiarity breeds esteem, not just for the story itself, but also for the skill of its human author. Both are reasons the Emmaus story is one of my favorites in all of Scripture.

My journey toward story

I haven't always known what a story is. Nor have I always known that I didn't know.

My journey as a Christian, pastor, missionary, and Bible teacher winds through life experiences going back as far as I can remember. I grew up in church, the type of church that held services Sunday mornings, Sunday nights, and Wednesday nights. My parents also took me to Sunday school each week. So, from a very young age, I learned Bible stories, especially stories about Jesus from the Gospels. My teachers used flannel graphs and object lessons to capture my attention. And I loved every minute.

But as I grew older, I hungered for a deeper understanding of truth. So I thought I had to turn away from story.

In high school, I approached my youth leaders and begged them to teach us Bible doctrine, but they didn't do it. I don't fault them; they were doing the best they could.

Once in Bible college, I fell in love with theology and the logic of my faith. I learned to outline Bible content, do words studies, and "theologize" everything. I listened to guest preachers in chapel. I observed as they unpacked their texts with alliterated outlines, parallel construction of their main points, and a poem or illustration at the end.

Still, I can remember only one sermon outline from this time. The preacher was a former pastor turned leader of a national fellowship of churches. His name was Dr. Paul Tassell. He preached through the book of Jonah one night for our Winter Bible Conference using this 4-point outline:

Chapter 1 - Jonah made the sea sick

Chapter 2 - Jonah made the whale sick

Chapter 3 - Jonah made Nineveh sick

Chapter 4 - Jonah made God sick

As a funny aside, I had heard Dr. Tassell preach this sermon earlier in my youth and had written the outline into the margins of my Bible. I had shared the outline with a fellow student who was having trouble with an assignment in one of our classes. She copied Dr. Tassell's outline from my Bible and turned it in as her own. Fortunately, our professor did not attend the conference that night. Still, I could hardly control my laughter as Dr. Tassell announced each point. Years later, Dr. Tassell and I became friends. I told him about my classmate and her use of his outline, which gave him a good laugh too.

After Bible college, I became a pastor. It was my turn to produce and preach through outlines of Bible texts Sunday in, Sunday out, and Wednesdays, too. I don't remember any of these outlines either. But I remember laboring to craft them. For inspiration, I would recall the two summers I apprenticed with a preacher known for his alliterations. I wanted to preach like him. But then I became more concerned with communicating out of my heart. Meanwhile, the aha-moments in God's Word kept coming. And once again, I loved it.

One day, I targeted the Book of Acts as a sermon series I could teach from a story perspective. Back then, I was reluctant to use the word story. Narrative sounded so much more theological. Story sounded childish, like something a Sunday school teacher might share with flannel graph. In time, I came to embrace story as the most descriptive term for a certain type of Bible content, including the overarching epic of Jesus Christ, the Son of God.

As I looked for tools to help me study the Book of Acts as narrative, I came across a book by Douglas Buckwalter, entitled The Character and Purpose of Luke's Christology. This book changed my life and the course of my preaching and teaching ministry. Buckwalter not only clarifies the theological bridge between Luke's Gospel and the Book of Acts, he also provides a story framework for both books. The aha-moments I gained felt like I was star-gazing on a clear night. It was the same exhilaration, the same deep moving in my heart I had experienced in my earliest encounter with Romans 8:28-29. I remember it now in vivid detail, as though it had just happened.

After Buckwalter and Acts, I began combing through other literature for more insights into Bible narrative. I found a lot on the rhetorical tools Bible writers used to craft their stories, but not much more. Soon I gave up.

Then, after 35 years of serving churches in the States, my wife and I became missionaries to Asia and the Indo-Pacific. Our time there, especially among the Japanese, convinced us of the need for a story approach to gospel messaging. The Japanese didn't understand the logic behind the messaging we were used to. So we expanded our messaging to tell more of Jesus' story. During that time, we began to study the mechanics, structure, and effects of story. Much of the literature we read was secular and meant for budding writers. But soon we found explanations of the science of story. These deepened my love for stories in God's Word. They also clarified what makes a story a story and why stories can be such moving and memorable ways of communicating.

Definition

The word story is an empty container you can fill with almost any meaning. Some use story to denote a news report, or to recount what happened yesterday, or to call out a lie. Others have in mind a movie plot, a novel, the lyrics of a song, a parable from the Bible, or any of a dozen other narrative forms, all of them stuffed into the letters s-t-o-r-y.

To make matters worse, the word story, unlike other familiar words, has no useful contrasting word to pair with to improve our understanding. It makes sense to pair black with white, hot with cold, day with night, etc. But no such pairing word seems to fit story. The thesaurus app on my phone lists fifty synonyms for story, but only one contrasting word, nonfiction, which doesn't always apply.

Narrative is a word that people often confuse with story. In fact, narrative is the first word many dictionaries use to define story. But for our purposes, we'll use the word narrative in a broader sense to label one of the three genres of literature found in Scripture. The others are poetry and prose discourse.

Some scholars estimate that half of the Bible falls into the genre of narrative. That helps, but doesn't clarify what we mean by Bible story. Keep in mind the empty container problem. We must narrow our understanding for the sake of clarity. Thus, I offer the definition of story proposed by author and researcher Kendall Haven in his book *Story Proof*:

A story is a detailed, character-based narration of a character's struggles to overcome obstacles and reach an important goal

Notice Kendall takes us into the specific elements of *story*. These are:

a character

a character's goal

a motive that makes the goal important

obstacles that must be overcome

details that bring everything together

A narrative may not stand as *story* if only one or two elements are present. For example, consider the bare bones report in Genesis 5:24 of Enoch's disappearance:

Enoch walked with God, and he was not, for God took him.

This report stands as a snippet of narrative. But some of Kendall's elements go missing. The report provides only the characters and a summary of what happened.

Stand-alone bits of dialogue are another example. Some are quite brief. So we might not expect them to contain all of Kendall's elements. But consider the lengthier dialogue between God and Noah in Genesis 6-9. As you read it, see if you can determine which story elements are present and which are missing. When I read it, for example, I see a main character—Noah. I see a goal—to build the ark. I see a motive—to survive the flood. But I do not see the mention of an obstacle standing in Noah's way.*

A final caveat concerns parables. Some parables stand as stories, others do not. For example, the parable of the mustard seed doesn't contain the elements of character, goal, etc. The lack doesn't make it any less powerful; just not a story.

Back to Emmaus

In closing, I want to take one more look at Kendall's definition:

A story is a detailed, character-based narration of a character's struggles to overcome obstacles and reach an important goal

Now let's revisit Luke 24:13-53 to determine whether a story is there. Does it qualify?

Story Deep

The answer is a definite *Yes!* Luke 24:13-53 offers a detailed account of two disciples (main-characters), who struggle to continue in their faith, because they witnessed Jesus' suffering and crucifixion, but not his resurrection (a major obstacle).

A story deep analysis of Genesis 6-9 would reveal that *all* of Haven's story elements are present, if we consider the commentary that other Bible texts add. I will offer this analysis in a future publication.

Chapter 2

Ask Story Questions

In my sophomore year of Bible college, I took a required course called *Principles and Methods of Bible Study*, taught by the same professor mentioned last chapter. In the course, I learned a knock-down version of the inductive method of Bible study. I call it a knock-down version, because there were only three steps instead of the five or six I'll share later. The three were: *Observation*, *Interpretation*, and *Application*.

Under the banner of *Observation*, one of our first assignments was to write fifty observations from the Great Commission of Matthew 28:18-20. When we finished, the professor said, "That's great. Now write fifty more."

The assignment stretched us, for sure. But the one-hundred observations we made had nothing to do with *story*. They focused instead on word meanings and grammar, the type of observations we could turn into deep-dive word studies, or sermon outlines. That's not what we're doing here.

Once we *Read the Story*, the next step is *Ask Story Questions*. When I read the Emmaus story, these questions stand out right away:

Why were the disciples heading to Emmaus?

Why didn't they stay in Jerusalem beyond the morning of the third day?

Does Emmaus, as a location, hold any significance?

What is the significance of the distance between Emmaus and Jerusalem?

Why were the eyes of the two disciples kept from recognizing Jesus?

Why did Luke name only one of the two disciples?

Was one of the two a woman?

Why did Jesus call them "fools" and "slow of heart?"

Why did Jesus act like he was going on once they came near Emmaus?

Why did Jesus taking bread, blessing it, breaking it, and giving it to the two disciples lead to their eyes being opened?

Why did Jesus vanish once the two disciples recognized him?

What did the disciples mean about their hearts burning in them?

Why was the resurrected Jesus hungry?

Why did he need to ask the disciples for something to eat?

Why did Jesus lead the group out to Bethany in the end?

How does the meaning of this story apply to life now?

Questions such as these arise naturally in connection to the *story* of the two disciples. Kendall Haven calls this the Make Sense Mandate. It's the God-created drive to make story sense of the information our brains take in. (Note: Kendall doesn't refer to God; that comes from my understanding of Scripture.)

Neuroscience and story

The latest neuroscience research shows that our subconscious minds use story categories to organize incoming information. That's why I describe the Make Sense Mandate as a God-created drive to make story sense. If the information we take in doesn't make story sense, we ignore it. Or we fill in with information, right or wrong, from pools of information that already exist in our minds. We create our own story.

An Apple iPhone is a powerful illustration of this way of mental processing. When I type a *w* to begin a text message, my phone "guesses" which word I have in mind. For example, I want to type the word *whale*. After typing the *w*, my phone guesses the word *what*. And if I'm not paying attention, that's the word it fills in. Who among us hasn't been too quick to press <send>, only to realize we just sent a message with the wrong word inserted? Perhaps an embarrassing one at that?

Our brains work in a similar way. If we allow them, our brains will "guess" and fill in information, whether the information is true or not. This is one of many reasons we must be intentional about asking story questions. Our skill in doing this grows as we become familiar with the craft of story. We'll learn more about the tools storytellers employ to share or withhold information. Their tactics for shaping their characters, and their characters' goals and motives, will become more obvious; as will the obstacles and conflict, risk and danger, and sequence of story events.

God has indeed hard-wired our brains to make story sense of the information we take in. Not just the information we read in the Bible, but information from all sources.

Neuroscience recognizes eight sensory inputs into the mind. The first five are well known: sight, hearing, taste, smell, and touch. The remaining three are not so well known. The first of these is interoception. Interoception refers to your perception of signals sent to the brain from within the body. For example, it's possible for you to perceive your heart beating in your chest. You might conclude from what you perceive that something's wrong, or that everything is ok. The second less well known sensory input is mental activity, which refers to emotions and thoughts, and to hopes, dreams, and memories. The third of the three is interconnectedness, which refers to our relationships, both with other people and with God.

The subconscious mind takes information from the eight sensory inputs and organizes it into story categories. Next, the subconscious mind takes this organized information and passes it on to the conscious mind. Think of a time when a friend made you question his motives. Motive is a core element of story. So as you wonder about motive, your subconscious and conscious minds work together to make sense of the words you heard, the non-verbal cues you observed, and anything else that comes to you through your other senses. Every bit contributes to your "conclusion" about motive. These are the findings of neuroscience. Research has shown that even infants respond to the story category of motive. It's the way God's made us.

Goals for asking

God's design thus summarized warrants our asking story questions. As we ask, we have three goals in mind.

The first is to satisfy curiosity. This goal comes first because of its tie to how we process information. Just as we muse over the motives of others, so we also muse over information missing from the other categories of story. Our desire to fill these categories runs deep. We call this desire *curiosity*.

The second goal is to raise the mind's subconscious activity to a conscious level. We learn how to attend to other things that happen on a subconscious level, such as when our hearts beat more rapidly, or when our breathing becomes more shallow. Similarly, we can learn to attend to our mind's processing of story information. One way to do this is to become intentional about asking story questions.

The third goal is to fill in with information that comes from the story. Keep in mind, if the word *whale* did not already exist in my phone's database, my phone wouldn't be able to suggest it. My phone can only suggest what it already knows. Rather than taking the chance that our minds have filled in with inaccurate information, we should seek whatever new information is required to satisfy the *Make Sense Mandate* with truth.

Take a second look at the story questions emerging from the Emmaus story:

Why were the disciples heading to Emmaus?

Why didn't they stay in Jerusalem beyond the morning of the third day?

Does Emmaus, as a location, hold any significance?

What is the significance of the distance between Emmaus and Jerusalem?

Why were the eyes of the two disciples kept from recognizing Jesus?

Why did Luke name only one of the two disciples?

Was one of the two a woman?

Why did Jesus call them "fools" and "slow of heart?"

Why did Jesus act like he was going on once they came near Emmaus?

Why did Jesus taking bread, blessing it, breaking it, and giving it to the two disciples lead to their eyes being opened?

Why did Jesus vanish once the two disciples recognized him?

What did the disciples mean about their hearts burning in them?

Why was the resurrected Jesus hungry?

Why did he need to ask the disciples for something to eat?

Why did Jesus lead the group out to Bethany in the end?

How does the meaning of this story apply to life now?

It isn't enough to have goals for asking questions. We also need a process for answering them, a process most likely to produce answers that are both helpful and accurate. Once again, Traina and Bauer:

> In general, the inductive process is whatever is most effective and efficient in determining the meaning of the text....
>
> Bauer, David R.; Traina, Robert A.. Inductive Bible Study (p. 20). Baker Publishing Group. Kindle Edition.

Some study processes fall short of Bauer and Traina's standard. Some do more harm than good. In chapter 5, I'll explain where the use of logical outlines fits on this scale. But first, I need to introduce you to additional story-related vocabulary in the next chapter.

Chapter 3

Take Notice of Story Elements

When we first encounter a story in the Bible, the default tendency for many of us is to look for any theological propositions we might find there. That reflects our training. Or what others have modeled for us. But neither of these means it's the right way to begin. The right way is with a *story deep* analysis. We otherwise risk misconstruing what the story is about, or missing it altogether.

As we noted in Chapters 1 and 2, a *story deep* analysis of Bible stories begins with reading the story and then asking story questions. The next step is to identify any story elements that stand out. Just about anything you find in a Bible story counts as a story element. But so we don't get bogged down, we'll focus here on elements most likely to factor into our analysis.

The first story element I attempt to discern is the story's main character. Then I look for the main character's goal, and the motive that makes the main character's goal matter. Next, I look for the antagonist, or the obstacle that blocks the main character's ability to reach his or her goal. I also search for what might serve as the story's inciting incident. But I do this aware that I may have to adjust my thinking as I continue.

I often also skim a story for its impact character. This is someone who influences the main character's choices as the story moves to its climax. In the Emmaus story, Jesus fills this role. Jesus also fills the role of an antagonist in the beginning.

Here's my analysis of story elements from the Emmaus story.

> **Main characters** — the two disciples in the first half of the story; plus the eleven in the second half

> **Goal or Object of Desire** — return to Emmaus to stay

> A main character's goal, or object of desire, may function over more than one level. The first level may be something that's clear; such as the disciples wanting to return to Emmaus. The second level may lie below the surface and connect the main character to a much deeper desire. To identify the first type of goal, ask WHAT physical thing does the main character want or want to happen? To identify the second, ask WHY?

> For these disciples on the road to Emmaus, their surface goal is to return to the actual village of Emmaus. But why? What is the deeper reason for their desire to return? Is there something below the surface here that requires some digging on my part? These are story questions I don't want to leave unanswered.

> **Motive** — This is where, in time, we will slot an answer to the WHY question.

> **Antagonist** — My first inclination is to say that Jesus is the antagonist; but, for now, I can't say how or why he blocks the two disciples.

In a story like the two disciples on the road to Emmaus, I am able right away to identify a few story elements, like the main characters and the antagonist. But as I go on, I'm not as clear on the others. For example, what is the story's inciting incident? Who is the impact character? What is the risk and danger? When I try to answer these, I run into the story questions I listed earlier. Perhaps, with a few others added in.

Not wanting to stop just yet, I expand my search to look for other kinds of story elements. For example, I search for any rhetorical devices that Bible writers used to craft their stories. These devices can lead to answers and meanings that lie hidden beneath the surface of the text. I also ponder ways to summarize what I can observe so far.

Below is an alphabetical listing of other story elements and related techniques I look for. A detailed discussion of each one is beyond the scope of what we're doing now. So I'm including just a brief description of each. Perhaps I will expand on these in a future publication. Here is my list (with an explanatory comment or two as warranted):

Action/Reaction

A study of the actions and reactions of characters sheds light on the subtexts in play. In remaining parts of my analysis of the Emmaus story, I will show how. I will also show why this story element is a critical part of any *story deep* analysis.

Characterization

Characterization refers to the art of portraying the traits and abilities of a character through:

(1) direct statement

(2) actions performed/not performed by a character

(3) reactions performed/not performed by a character (especially reactions to conflict and adversity)

(4) dialogue

(5) foils (parallel or contrasting characters and their actions)

(6) character relationships

(7) tone

Storytellers use characterization to foster empathy and sympathy for their characters, or distance and ill will.

In the Emmaus story, Luke's characterization of the two disciples makes us feel their initial disappointment over not seeing Jesus. We know what it's like to not see Jesus. That can be just as disappointing for us.

Through sympathy with the two disciples, Luke also invites us to ponder their confusion. Jesus said he would rise again, so why didn't he appear? We can understand why they would become confused. We also wonder why the two disciples didn't recognize Jesus when he first appeared to them. They had seen Jesus prior to his death. Why didn't they recognize him?

Direct speech

Direct speech includes both the said and the unsaid. Both could factor into our *story deep* analysis of the Emmaus story.

Dramatic irony

Dramatic irony involves knowledge that writers share with their audience but not with their characters. Characters may simply not know, or hold to what the audience knows is a false belief. Either way, the irony of their ignorance or false belief creates tension and moves the plot forward. For example, Luke informs his readers that the stranger who joins the disciples is Jesus. But he doesn't inform the disciples. They longed to see Jesus resurrected. Then, when he appeared, they didn't recognize him. Luke calls attention to the irony of this by ensuring that everyone else knows who the stranger is.

Impact Character

An impact character influences a main character's choices in the story's climax. He or she may give advice, or otherwise constrain what the main character chooses. God plays the role of impact character in some stories, though perhaps "behind the scenes."

In the Emmaus story, Jesus is the impact character. Jesus also functions as a bit of an antagonist at first.

Juxtaposition

Juxtaposition is the act of placing items close to each other for comparison.

In the story of the two disciples, Luke juxtaposes Jerusalem and Emmaus. Jerusalem is a large city; Emmaus, a small village. Jerusalem is at the center of God's promises; Emmaus, on the outskirts. Jerusalem means keeping the faith; Emmaus, giving up.

Logline

A logline summarizes a story in one sentence. Some call this sentence a story's concept. Others call it a story's hook or elevator pitch.

A typical logline follows this convention:

[A main character described with an adjective or by a social role] [action the main character must take] to [overcome adversity] or [fulfill an important goal].

I'll flesh out this formula for the Emmaus story in due time. I refer to the formula here, because sometimes I draft a logline as I begin a *story deep* analysis. This early draft functions more like a "logline hypothesis," as I carry my analysis forward.

Motif

A motif is a recurring theme. Motifs may reveal other dynamics at work.

No particular motif stands out at this point in the Emmaus story. However, our story-deep analysis will point in the end to a motif featured both here and elsewhere in Luke's writings.

Names (of both people and places)

The meanings of names often, perhaps always, factors into the analysis of Bible stories.

We are told the name of only one of the two disciples on the road to Emmaus. Why is that?

Narration

Bible stories often use narration for irony and repetition.

Numbers

Numbers in Bible stories can carry significance beyond just the quantities they represent (for example, 666).

The numbers that appear in the Emmaus story do not appear to carry any symbolic meaning.

Plot

Plot is the design of a story's sequence of events moving from conflict to resolution.

Plot conflict

Plot conflict refers to the central struggle of a plot. This can be physical, mental, or emotional. It can also be moral or spiritual.

Repetition

Bible writers use repetition for emphasis.

In the Emmaus story, Luke has Jesus tell his story from Old Testament Scriptures twice. This repetition will factor into our analysis.

Setting

Time, place, and other similar details form a story's setting.

In Luke 24:13, the Emmaus story is said to take place on the "very day" of Jesus' resurrection. This timeframe sets the story within the Feast of Unleavened Bread.

Thema and Rhema

Thema are words an author assumes you already know. Rhema are words an author clarifies within a story. We will notice both in the Emmaus story.

For more information on Thema and Rhema, see the Introduction in *The Pentateuch as Narrative* by John Sailhamer.

Time

The time element of a story matters. Bible writers can "skip" dozens, if not hundreds, of years in a single sentence. Or they can use dozens of verses, even chapters, to zero in on the details of some happening.

Tone

Tone refers to the attitude that a storyteller takes toward his or her subject.

Type-scene

Type-scenes are like master plots. They feature certain types of characters and archetypal plots. One example is a betrothal type-scene. Hebrew scholar Robert Alter, explains:

> The betrothal type-scene, then, must take place with the future bridegroom, or his surrogate, having journeyed to a foreign land. There he encounters a girl—the term "na'arah" invariably occurs unless the maiden is identified as so-and-so's daughter—or girls at a well. Someone, either the man or the girl, then draws water from the well; afterward, the girl or girls rush to bring home the news of the stranger's arrival (the verbs "hurry" and "run" are given recurrent emphasis at this junction of the type-scene); finally, a betrothal is concluded between the stranger and the girl, in the majority of instances, only after he has been invited to a meal.

Alter, Robert. The Art of Biblical Narrative (p. 62). Basic Books. Kindle Edition.

Many Bible stories conform to some or all of the expectations of a type-scene. The Emmaus story does not appear to be one of them.

Unifying action

Unifying action summarizes the core action a protagonist takes to reach his or her goal. This is like a logline.

The entries above do not form a complete list of all story elements. I included them to provide helpful guidance for our story deep analysis. I also included them to signal that analyzing Bible stories isn't always a linear process. We don't have complete certainty about each at this point. So we may return to these items to apply information we've uncovered elsewhere. The entries also show how much ground there is to cover in a story deep analysis of Bible stories. We're just getting started.

Chapter 4

Logical Outlines

During the second semester of my sophomore year at Bible college, I had the same professor I mentioned before for a second class: *John and Romans*. On the first day of class, the professor came through the door, strode over to a podium at the front, and opened the class in prayer. In less than thirty seconds, we were full on into the start of his lecture.

The professor had an intimidating way about him, though you might not have guessed that based on his appearance. He wore black thick-rimmed glasses with tinted lenses, as though he needed to protect his eyes from the glare of the pages upon pages of commentaries spread across the desk in his office.

The professor started the class by reviewing the syllabus. Based on the title of the class, you'd think it was the professor's plan for us to spend the first half of the semester studying John's story about Jesus; and the second half, Paul's treatise to the church in Rome. But you'd be only partially correct. And in this professor's class, "partially correct" never translated to a grade much higher than a C.

Our first class project involved creating a title for each chapter in John, and then a more detailed outline of Romans. Now I'm pretty sure that neither John nor Paul wrote their portions of the Scriptures in chapter/verse format. But that didn't stop us. And neither did the fact that several chapters in John contain more than one story. At least in Romans, we were free to follow the logical flow of Paul's argument. But creating chapter titles for a narrative portion of Scripture like the

Gospel of John reinforced an expectation that we brought to Bible college with us. It was a sense that outlines, of whatever kind, Roman numerals, or chapter titles—outlines are a preferred way to classify data in all genres of Bible texts.

A second tool, preferred with equal enthusiasm, was *word study*. By *word study*, I mean the practice that begins with choosing a word to study. Next you look up the word in an expository dictionary. Then check the word's usage in other passages. Finally, you plug the nuances of its meanings back into the texts where the word appears. Although such studies have their place, they turn your attention away from story questions, or other units of analysis, such as clauses and complete sentences.

This doesn't make word studies bad. But the person using them needs to be aware of the danger.

Outlines don't work

For analyzing Bible stories as story, most types of outlines are never up to the task. I'm not sure why anyone ever thought they would be.

Notice I wrote *most types of outlines*. Perhaps you remember the term *step-outline* from the Introduction. That is something very different. The type of outline I have in mind now is a Roman numeral outline, or some variation thereof. Apple's Pages calls it a Harvard outline. These types of outlines have nothing to do with analyzing stories as *story*. They're meant instead to analyze and communicate the logical structure of discourse. No matter how clever they are, they distract from our focus on the elements of story.

I want to illustrate the point using the story of *Goldilocks and the Three Bears*. What would a Roman numeral outline of a story like *Goldilocks and the Three Bears* look like? Check this out:

I. The Bears and their Porridge

    A. A Large Portion

    B. A Lunch Portion

    C. A Little Portion

II. Goldilocks and her Palate

    A. Goldilocks Tempted

    B. Porridge Tasted

    C. Chairs Tested

    D. Beds Tainted

III. The Bears and their Preoccupation

    A. The Curiosity of the Bears

    B. The Concern of the Bears

    C. The Confrontation of the Bears

IV. Goldilocks and her Precipitance

    A. Goldilocks Awakes

    B. Goldilocks Alights

    C. Goldilocks Abandons

© 2022 Randal Gilmore

It's funny because it's such a ridiculous way to treat a story like *Goldilocks and the Three Bears*. If you have children or grandchildren young enough, and they've never heard the story, try sharing the outline with them and watch their reaction. Start by saying you're going to tell them a story. Then tell them the outline. If they're younger, they'll move on to something else. And if they're old enough, you won't get far before they give you a look like, "What are you talking about?"

No matter the alliteration or how much detail and parallelism, stories are not meant to be outlined. Not with Roman numeral outlines. This includes stories found in Scripture.

In Inductive Bible Study, Traina and Bauer offer thirteen guidelines for using logical outlines, explaining that logical outlines are better suited for studying discourse literature:

[The logical outline] ...simply serves as a tool by which to trace logical development, to discover how various thoughts are related to each other, to determine what is primary and what is secondary, and to ascertain the conclusion toward which the author is moving.

Bauer, David R.; Traina, Robert A.. Inductive Bible Study (p. 400). Baker Publishing Group. Kindle Edition.

Traina and Bauer's thirteenth guideline reads:

Prepare an outline only after thorough study, and let it be a means of summarizing your study. If one has studied a passage well, it ought to fall into an outline of its own accord. One should not be concerned about outlining as such during the process of interpretation.

Bauer, David R.; Traina, Robert A.. Inductive Bible Study (p. 402). Baker Publishing Group. Kindle Edition.

We should inscribe this guideline on a plaque and hang it up for everyone to see. After all, think of the last time you used a logical outline to tell the story, not just report on your study. But don't be too hard on yourself. Most of us have chosen logical outlines as our go-to Bible study method, regardless of which genre a passage falls into, because of our training. So I'm not judging. This is not about the righteousness of our intentions.

Bible outlines website

Recently, I found a website that features outlines of Bible content. It includes outlines of story content. The owner and creator of the site is well meaning to be sure. Here's his rationale for the site:

In an age where Bible doctrine and sermons and theology have been saddled with negative connotations, I am driven to elevate the objective truth of God's Word above the shallowness and limited perspective of our own subjective experiences. The ultimate goal is not warehousing knowledge (which puffs up) but defining the proper boundaries for our love and obedience so that our relationship with our Lord Jesus Christ is on His revealed terms. Idolatry is making God after our own image and trying to approach Him on our own terms.

I fear that too many believers today have been sucked into some type of "Bible-lite" context where their spiritual diet consists of junk food rather than steak and potatoes. I am weary of a steady diet of topical messages where the preacher comes up with "Four Points About X" and then strings together the appropriate Scriptural passages to support the observations he wants to hammer home. Usually the speaker is constrained by the limits of his existing knowledge of the Scriptures – that is how he arrived at his observations. Often the various contexts of the passages are ignored or misrepresented in this approach. Inductive study conducted in a systematic fashion that tracks through a book of the Bible paragraph by paragraph has far greater possibilities of opening up new lines of truth and presenting the balanced picture that the author intended.

https://www.bibleoutlines.com/about (accessed May 24, 2022)

I couldn't agree more. But tied to his use of logical outlines in the rest of the website, I also recognize three very dangerous false beliefs in the subtext of these words.

The first is that only logical outlines can lift us up from the mire of subjective experience. No other Bible study method works.

I could write an entire book in response to this false belief. Stories in the Bible point to objective truths through the subjective experiences of their characters. Therefore, to understand the objective truth that comes out of a story, we must first understand the subjective experience of its characters. The best way to do this is to study a story as *story*. This means not using a logical outline to analyze a story's content.

The second false belief is that the study of Bible stories as *story* means giving less emphasis to doctrine. This false belief extends from the first. But this time it's tied to a fear of turning away from theological depth; as though turning to story as *story* means turning away from theological depth. In this book, one of my goals is to show you theological insights gained through a *story deep* analysis.

The third false belief is that using logical outlines is the only path to inductive study— all other Bible study methods fall short. The ramifications of this false belief are serious to be sure. Therefore, I'll take time in a later section of this chapter to detail what the inductive method of study is. I'll also show that how it applies to a *story deep* analysis. Meanwhile, I want to show the logical outline of the Emmaus story offered in Bibleoutlines.com.

A Logical Outline of the Emmaus Story

I.   (24:13-16) Spiritual blindness requires divine enlightenment

    A. (:13) Trip to Emmaus - In the vicinity of the Key events of the crucifixion and the resurrection

    B. (:14) Talk about recent events concerning Jesus in Jerusalem - Inquiring about the key events

    C. (:15) Travel companion - In the presence of the key figure - the risen messiah himself

    D. (:16) Thwarted from recognizing Jesus - In total spiritual darkness

II. (24:17-24) Only Jesus can resolve our spiritual confusion and despair

(:17) Jesus Invites Our Spiritual Questions

    A. (:18-21) Confusion concerning Jesus' Messianic redemptive mission

       1. (:18-20) Clarity needed regarding the crucifixion of Jesus Christ

          a. (:18) Ironic question

          b. (:19a) Inquisitive response

          c. (:19b-20) Irreconcilable tension

             i. (:19b) Jesus looked like the Messiah

             ii. (:20) Jesus was crucified by the Jewish religious leaders

       2. (:21) Clarity needed regarding the Messianic redemptive mission of Jesus Christ

          a. Hope of Israel's redemption

          b. Disappointment over his death

B. (:22-24) Confusion concerning the empty tomb and the resurrection
   1. (:22-23) Testimony of the women raised questions
   2. (:24) Testimony of our companions raised questions

III. (24:25-27) We must listen in faith to the exposition of Jesus in the Scriptures

   A. (:25) Reprimand over failure to believe the messianic message of OT prophets
   B. (:26) Reinforcement of the essential link between Christ's suffering and glory
   C. (:27) Revelation of Christ in the OT

IV. (24:28-35) Divine enlightenment—The opening of our eyes to see Jesus—confirms the resurrection

   A. (:28-29) The blessing of being with Jesus
      1. (:28) Opportunity almost lost
      2. (:29a) Opportunity pursued
      3. (:29b) Opportunity realized
   B. (:30-31) The blessing of truly seeing Jesus
      1. (:30) Truly seeing Jesus is a gift from God associated with genuine fellowship
      2. (:31) Truly seeing Jesus physically confirmed the reality of the resurrection
   C. (:32) The blessing of divine spiritual illumination and exposition of Scripture
   D. (:33-34) Testimony of the disciples to the resurrection
   E. (:35) Confirming testimony of the Emmaus Road disciples

https://www.bibleoutlines.com/blog/luke-2413-35-opening-eyes-on-the-road-to-emmaus Accessed May 17, 2022

I didn't include this outline here just to pick it apart. Still, I need to make a few observations that I hope will stand out even more after we've finished working through the process of a *story deep* analysis.

First, notice the attempts within each of the outline's main points to employ alliteration and parallelism. All of the second level points under the first main point begin with the letter *T*. Under the second main point, they begin with the letter *C*. Under the third, the letter *R*. Under the fourth, the letter *T*. Many third and fourth level points are also alliterated. On every level, the alliterations seem forced, which often happens unless you're an uber-talented wordsmith. Even then, you end up using words that are obscure, like the word *Precipitance* in my outline of Goldilocks. Or words that don't line up with what's happening in the story. For example, take the word *Reinforcement* in point B of main point III. When Jesus tells the disciples the things concerning himself beginning with Moses and the Prophets, and in all the Scriptures, was he *reinforcing* something they already knew? Or was he *enlightening* them? The answer is obvious, but the word *Enlightenment* doesn't fit.

Keep in mind, a top reason for using logical outlines is supposed to be the pursuit of objective truth. But crafting them seems to work against this priority. Something else wins out. Often, it's the value of consistency. In using *Reinforcement* in point B of main point III, consistency wins out. Alliteration and parallelism carry the day. But under main point II, clarity wins out, forcing the creator to insert an "orphan" point: "(:17) Jesus invites our spiritual questions."

Outlines like the one in our example also seem to change their unit of analysis at whim. Among the sub-points, the focus shifts back and forth from a single verse to phrases within a verse and to phrases within a verse plus the next verse. One reason for the shifting back and forth involves presupposing that chapter and verse divisions are more than markers to show where content appears in a text. The presumption is they also organize meaning. Thus, our analysis has to follow those divisions. Sometimes, of course, it doesn't pan out so neatly, forcing the outline creator to change the configuration to make a point.

The last observation I'll make concerns what vexes me most. An outline like the one in the example fails on many levels. Not the least is in summarizing the actual story that's told. Take another look at the outline's main points:

I. Spiritual blindness requires divine enlightenment
II. Only Jesus can resolve our spiritual confusion and despair
III. We must listen in faith to the exposition of Jesus in the Scriptures
IV. Divine enlightenment—The opening of our eyes to see Jesus—confirms the resurrection

These are interpretations of the story's content, not expositions. The word *our* embedded in each point reveals this. The story is not about "us" or "our." It's about the two disciples on the road to Emmaus. The outline creator skips past the actual story to outline the abstractions he reads into the text. Then he crafts applications, which he summarizes in outline form. These he represents as the text's objective truth.

In main point I, sub-point D, the outline creator writes: "Thwarted from recognizing Jesus - In total spiritual darkness." This too doesn't tell the actual story. Why were the disciples thwarted from recognizing Jesus? Because they were "in spiritual darkness"? What warrant is there for saying that? The actual story doesn't mention "spiritual darkness." It says nothing at all about a "spiritual" thwarting of the disciples from recognizing Jesus. It only says that their physical eyes "were kept from recognizing Jesus."

I could point to many other examples in the outline of failing to connect to the elements of story, or to the actual story itself. But I won't, because I'm confident that the *story deep* process will do that for me. Besides, someone might be clever enough to come up with an outline that sprinkles in story elements. But even then, I assure you, the most we could hope for from outlining Bible stories is something very different than the actual story the text is telling us.

Logical Outlines That Sprinkle in Story Elements

Years ago, I remember hearing a respected pastor, and excellent speaker, preach through the Old Testament story of Ahab and Naboth from 1 Kings 21. He offered an alliterated outline with four main points:

I. Ahab's Covetousness
II. Naboth's Conviction
III. Jezebel's Cruelty
IV. Elijah's Courage

To the pastor's credit, he did not use the outline to impose structure on the text verse by verse. He tried to tell the story that's there. But he missed. For one, there was no room in the pastor's outline for the story's ending when Ahab repented, prompting God to confide in Elijah that he would delay but still carry out judgment on the wicked king. This ending shows that the story is not about the four points in the pastor's outline. It's about the enduring relevance of the promises and threats that Jehovah made to the historical nation of Israel and its leaders. How do I know this? First, by recognizing that logical outlines are not the right tool to achieve a *story deep* analysis. Then, by examining the text's structure and details tied to what I know about story and story elements.

In the next chapter, we'll move on to take a closer look at the inductive method applied to a *story deep* analysis.

Chapter 5

The Inductive Method

In one sense, this chapter will serve as Part 2 of the previous chapter on the *story deep* method vs. logical outlines. In another, it stands on its own. I divided the two chapters to emphasize my explanation of the inductive method of Bible study. As noted in the last chapter, logical outlines have their place, but at the end of the inductive process. Using logical outlines at the outset of a study, using them to analyze Bible content, may turn out ok when the focus is discourse. When the focus is story, it almost never does. So it bears repeating: logical outlines are the wrong tool for analyzing Bible stories.

The right tool is the inductive method. Many falsely believe that we must set aside the inductive method to study Bible stories with a *story deep* method. But I believe their actual fear is what I call the Wild West of Bible interpretation, where everyone does what is right in his own eyes and duels against objective truth..

I understand the concern. During my initial trek into how to study Bible stories, I found little consistency of method among commentators. It did seem like the Wild West. Even conservative commentators were all over the map with their methods. But they shared one thing in common. None showed how to study Bible stories using an inductive method.

Still, I was determined to figure things out. I believe the inductive method applies to the study of Bible stories. It doesn't apply only when the content is discourse. It applies to the study of poetry too. And to the study of story.

The Inductive Method

Five steps are required in the inductive method of study. The first is observation of details, or collection of data. We know these data as "particulars." The next step is classification of the data. The third is deductions. These are hypotheses you test in the fourth step: verification. The fifth step is application.

Here are the steps in list form:

1. Collection of Data—gathering facts

2. Classification—putting the data in categories or into some type of order

3. Deduction—formulating logically valid hypotheses

4. Verification—checking to see whether our hypotheses hold true more generally

5. Application—which refers to pragmatics and how all of this informs what we should think and do

In the last chapter, I shared that I first learned about the inductive method in Bible college. However, my professors didn't teach all five steps. They collapsed the five into three: observation, interpretation, and application. I've listed all five here, because I think they offer a clearer picture of the inductive method. I also should mention the possibility of a sixth step: assumptions. Assumptions belong at the top of the list.

Back to Logical Outlines

You might ask why logical outlines aren't a good fit for an inductive analysis of stories. After all, isn't using a logical outline just another way of classifying data? The answer is, *Yes, it is*. But there are two problems.

First, just because you *can* use a logical outline doesn't mean it's the right tool. We all know it's possible to use tools to do jobs they're not designed to do. For example, you can use a hammer to drive a screw into a piece of wood. But a hammer isn't designed for that purpose.

Remember Traina and Bauer contend that logical outlines are designed to summarize findings at the *end* of an analytical process, not to classify the data at the *beginning*, or even somewhere in between.

The second problem is related to the first. There isn't a warrant for going beyond what Traina and Bauer say about the design and role of logical outlines. Back to the hammer and screw analogy, just because the idea to use a hammer pops into your head doesn't warrant its use in every instance. In contrast, the warrant for using a story deep method to analyze Bible stories rises from ties to the craft of storytelling. We use the same tools to analyze Bible stories that Bible writers used to write them. Even if the tools are not exactly the same, they're similar enough to validate the warrant. For example, Gospel writers used the tools of ancient "bios" to tell Jesus' story. Bios did not use all the tools of a more modern approach. It left out many of the details of family background and psychological description of its character. It focused instead on what a subject said and did so others could learn from him and live by his model. In spite of these differences, bios writers used many of the same storytelling techniques we use.

More on verification

I want to mention something now about the third step in the inductive process: deduction. This step leads to forming hypotheses. All hypotheses should be logical. They should also be verifiable. So we must test them. Keep in mind also, there's always the possibility that new data will emerge and disconfirm what we think at first.

For example, suppose you do a word study on the word *gospel*. First you collect the data, listing the 91 times the English word gospel appears in the New Testament. Next you classify the data, separating the 91 into five categories:

1. occurrences in the Gospels

2. in Acts

3. in Paul's writings

4. in Peter's writings

5. in John's writings (Revelation).

Next, you choose to go deeper into Paul's writings, because they contain the majority of the occurrences. You call to mind 1 Corinthians 15:1-4, where Paul seems to define the word gospel:

> Now I would remind you, brothers, of the gospel I preached to you, which you received, in which you stand, and by which you are being saved, if you hold fast to the word I preached to you—unless you believed in vain. For I delivered to you as of first importance what I also received: that Christ died for our sins in accordance with the Scriptures, that he was buried, that he was raised on the third day in accordance with the Scriptures.

You read what Paul wrote and hypothesize the meaning of the English word *gospel*:

> That Christ died for sins in accordance with the Scriptures, that he was buried, and that he was raised on the third day in accordance with the Scriptures

You hypothesize further that this is what the word gospel means, especially in the writings of Paul. You attempt to confirm this. If confirmed, you might be able to generalize the word's meaning to the other four categories in which the word appears. But then you come to Galatians 3:8, where Paul wrote:

> And the Scripture, foreseeing that God would justify the Gentiles by faith, preached the gospel beforehand to Abraham, saying, "In you shall all the nations be blessed."

In this verse, Paul infuses the word gospel with additional meaning. It's not only "that Christ died for our sins in accordance with the Scriptures, that he was buried, that he was raised on the third day in accordance with the Scriptures," as important as this is, but also the promise of blessing to all nations through Abraham. Now you must modify your hypothesis about the meaning of the word *gospel*, as it appears in the writings of Paul.

No matter what type of study we undertake, we will always need to verify our hypotheses to complete the inductive process. Even if our hypotheses seem to be so right at first.

Verification and the study of Bible stories

Verification plays a similar role as we apply the inductive method to our study of Bible stories. For example, the data for the story of the disciples on the road to Emmaus is found in Luke 24:13-53. The creator of bibleoutlines.com chooses, without warrant, to classify the data with a Roman numeral outline. The outline ends with verse 35 of chapter 24; with a separate outline offered for 24:36-53. The two outlines mean that their creator deduced that the story ends in verse 24:35, and a second story begins in 24:36. The outline creator also deduces certain things about the story's meaning that he writes into his outline's four main points. These deductions (as well as others featured in the outline) are subject to verification.

In a *story deep* analysis, we verify against three standards: (1) what we know about story as a genre; (2) internal and external consistency; and (3) the Make Sense Mandate. How we use these three will become clearer as you continue to study the *story deep* method.

Meanwhile, consider the outline creator's main point IV: "the opening of our eyes to see Jesus confirms the resurrection." If opening our eyes truly confirms the resurrection, why did doubts rise in the hearts of the eleven after Jesus appeared to them (24:38)? Besides, if that's what the story's about—confirming the resurrection by the opening of "our" eyes—how does that apply to us? Of what real value is such a deduction to us now? We have never seen Jesus, nor will we ever, not until we see him either in heaven, or at his return. I could go on here, but I think you get the idea. In the end, main point IV doesn't stand up against any of the three standards of verification. It violates what we know about story as a genre. It's inconsistent with what happens in other parts of the story. And it violates the Make Sense Mandate wired into our brains.

I could offer similar analysis of the outline creator's choice to end the story at Luke 24:35. Or of the remaining main points of his outline. Measured against the three standards, all the deductions/hypotheses tied to his choices are disconfirmed. Therefore, they should be modified or discarded.

Errant interpretations are possible, no matter which tool we use to analyze Bible stories. We must be humble enough to admit that. But we must also note the exceptional risk imposed by the use of logical outlines. They risk our misclassifying story data, which gives rise to deductions likely to be disconfirmed, especially when these deductions measure against the three standards: (1) what we know about story as a genre; (2) internal and external consistency; and (3) the Make Sense Mandate.

Now we know better

Before moving on, I want to return to Traina and Bauer's advice once more. Remember, they advise to wait until the end of the study process and use the outline to summarize your findings. This use of logical outlines isn't all bad, or always wrong. But it comes with the temptation, especially when Bible stories are involved, to shortcut the analytical process for the sake of "coming up with an outline" as quickly as possible. All of us know what it's like to yield to this temptation. I know I do. But now we know better: yielding risks leaving diamonds undiscovered. Or worse yet, talking ourselves into believing that we found diamonds that aren't actually there.

We'll keep this discussion going in the next chapter with *Check the Larger Story*.

Chapter 6

Check the Larger Story

Imagine going for a hike through an unfamiliar forest. You trudge past a dizzying number of trees and tramp through the undergrowth. You descend to cross shallow streams, then climb back to level ground. But the forest terrain has made it impossible for you to walk a straight line. You feel confused, turned around, unsure of the way out.

I know by experience how it feels to get lost in a deep and unfamiliar forest. I went deer hunting one time by myself in a large tract of Pennsylvania woods where I had never hunted before. In time, I realized I didn't know the way back to my car. By then, it was near the end of the day and the sun was going down. I could feel my heart racing as I admitted to myself that I was lost. Once I calmed down, I found a marked trail. I knew it would take me somewhere, so I followed it anyway. With the sun going down, I had no choice. When I emerged from the woods a few hours later, I was miles from where I had parked.

The next day, I studied a map of the area and determined how and where I went wrong. The map offered me a perspective from "above" all the trees and other features of the forest I stumbled through the night before. As much as I love to hike through woods like that, the terrain had disoriented me. As I stared at the map and reflected on what happened, I realized how true the familiar saying was: You can't see the forest for the trees.

(By the way, I also learned never again to go hunting by myself in unfamiliar territory.)

Individual Bible texts, whether stories or not, can stand like trees in an unfamiliar forest. Finding our way through requires us to rise above the forest and take it in as a whole. This is where story structure comes in.

A few years ago, I began referring to the larger story told in Scripture about Jesus as the Gospel Story-arc. I chose the word *arc* with intention, knowing that some people wouldn't know what it means. Some, when they hear it, think they're hearing *ark* instead of *arc*.

The word *arc* calls attention to the changes that take place in a story; changes in a story's main character, and in the charge of the story's core value. I'll say more about both in due time. For now, think of an arc as a visual metaphor for a story's journey of change. An arc's bending from its starting point to its end maps the journey. A story's timeline is a straight line, starting with what happens first—first this, then that, and so on to the end, a straight line.

So when I refer to Jesus' story as the Gospel Story-arc, I do not mean the historical timeline of events portrayed in Scripture. Nor do I mean the so-called list of ways that Jesus "appears" in each book of the Bible:

> In Genesis, he's the Creator and promised Redeemer
>
> In Exodus, he's the Passover Lamb
>
> In Leviticus, he's the High Priest
>
> In Numbers, he's water in the desert
>
> In Deuteronomy, he becomes the curse for us
>
> In Joshua, he is the Commander of the army of the Lord
>
> In Judges, he delivers us from injustice
>
> Etc.
>
> (https://www.biblestudytools.com/bible-study/topical-studies/in-every-book-of-the-bible.html accessed on May 25, 2022)

As creative and well-meaning as the person is who put this list together, there is no story here. There's only a list of abstractions tied to content found in each of the Bible's 66 books. In many cases, the the ties are weak and impose on a book's content.

The Gospel Story-arc

The Gospel Story-arc summary forms a story all by itself. It features all the elements of a story—a character with a goal, and a motive that makes the goal important; an antagonist; and risk and danger. It also features a structured sequence of events.

The structure of the summary forms a Freytag pyramid. Think of the word pyramid as a kind of arc. To the left is an upward slope leading to a pinnacle. To the right, a downward slope falls away from the pinnacle. This shape is used to plot seven elements of story: exposition; inciting incident; rising action; climax; falling action; resolution; and untying. A story's climax stands at the pinnacle. Exposition, the inciting incident, and rising action lead to the climax. From there, on the downward side, falling action, resolution, and untying slope away.

As I share Gospel Story-arc messaging below, for the sake of clarity, I will label each part according to it where it falls on Freytag's pyramid, and according to its divisions in Scripture.

Exposition (Genesis 1-2)

The God of the Bible is a great and eternal King over all. In the beginning,

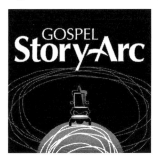

God created the heavens and the earth to be places where His rule would be fully honored and obeyed. Here is where God's Spirit began operating in the world, hovering over the face of the waters, energizing and empowering all things.

The first humans were the pinnacle of God's creation. He made them in His image and blessed them with four kinds of perfect relationships: (1) with Him;

(2) with each other; (3) with self; and (4) with the rest of creation. At the end of Creation Week, God saw everything He had made and declared it "very good."

God commanded Adam and Eve to multiply and fill the earth. He expected them to grow as His stewards in each of the four categories of relationships. God commanded them not to eat from the Tree of the Knowledge of Good and Evil. He warned them against the penalty of death if they disobeyed.

Inciting Incident (Genesis 3)

In time, Adam and Eve rebelled against God, choosing to disobey God in response to Satan's temptation. Satan posed as a beguiling serpent in a tree God planted in the Garden of Eden.

Adam and Eve's disobedience shattered the four perfect relationships, leading to the "death" God had warned them about.

God announced curses on the very things he said earlier were "very good." These curses reveal that the death God threatened not only meant physical death but also shame and strife, pain and suffering, and the spread of evil and unbelief.

Within the curse announced against the serpent, God promised to put down the rebellion through "the Seed of the Woman", a virgin-born Savior and King.

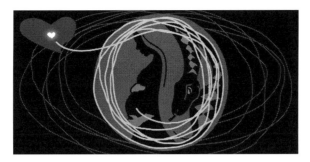

God's promise showed that humanity would divide into two sides from then on: the side of the serpent vs. the side of the Seed of the Woman. Each side would reflect the character of its representative. Sin and death, shame and relational strife, pain and suffering, and the spread of evil and unbelief, would mark the side of the serpent. Righteousness and life, integration and relational harmony would mark the side of the Seed of the Woman. Victory over pain and suffering would mark it also, along with faith, love, and obedience toward God. Thus, the side of the Seed of the Woman would reflect the blessing and goodness of God's rule in life overall, including the four categories of relationships.

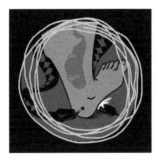

God's curse against the serpent also pointed to an epic battle someday between the serpent and the Seed of the Woman. God said that the serpent would "bruise the heel" of the Seed of the Woman. This meant the Seed of the Woman would experience significant pain and suffering, and possibly death.

But God also showed that the Seed of the Woman would prevail; he would "bruise the head" of the serpent. In the end, God's promise of deliverance through the Seed of the Woman meant that someday He would restore the earth as a place where His rule is fully honored and obeyed.

After the curses, God foreshadowed forgiveness through the shed blood of an innocent substitute, applied to everyone who by faith comes onto the side of the Seed of the Woman.

The rest of human history is the unfolding of God's plan for restoration through the Seed of the Woman.

Rising Action (Genesis 4-Malachi)

Over time, God narrowed the family line of the Seed of the Woman to Seth, then Noah, Shem, Abraham, Isaac, and Jacob (Israel). God also reassured these men and others that He would follow through on His plan.

God chose the descendants of Jacob and formed them into the nation of Israel, using just 613 laws. God intended for Israel to showcase the blessings of living directly under His rule. He conditioned his blessing of future generations of Israel on their obedience to his laws.

Meanwhile, God also planned for Israel to function as a "kingdom of priests." He would bless other nations through Israel, so long as they too blessed Israel. This stipulation stood on top of others God spelled out for all nations by his covenant with Noah and his sons after the Flood.

As time moved on, God revealed more about the promised Seed of the Woman. He would be born without the agency of a human father. God would be his father, giving him the nature of both God and man. Thus, the promised one would be King. He also would be a prophet and priest.

Over thousands of years, the line of the Seed of the Woman was narrowed further to the tribe of Judah, and then to the house of David the King.

The glory of David's kingdom reached its zenith under the rule of David's son, Solomon. But the Seed of the Woman would someday prove to be an even greater son of David. The glory of his kingdom would soar to even greater heights.

After Solomon, the nation of Israel began spiraling downward. They failed to live up to their covenants with God. So God withdrew his presence and blessing. But God showed that this period of withdrawal would be of limited duration. Then he would renew and exceed the previous blessing on Israel, and on all nations through Israel, under the rule of the promised Seed of the Woman.

Climax (Matthew 1 - Acts 1)

Many years later, Jesus of Nazareth was born in Bethlehem, the city of David. Jesus claimed to be the Deliverer, the promised prophet, priest, and king. God authenticated Jesus and his claims through the miracle of the virgin birth, along with the many signs and wonders he performed during his life on earth.

Still, the leaders of Israel rejected Jesus, as did many of their followers, leading them to arrest and execute him. Jesus' suffering and death on the Cross was the "bruising of the heel" predicted long ago. It was only a "bruising" since Jesus was had the power to conquer death by his resurrection from the dead on the third day. God the Father raised Jesus to new life.

Forty days later, he exalted Jesus at his right hand as Lord of lords.

Falling Action (Acts 2 - Revelation 5)

From this exalted position, Jesus began building His church, which comprises people he has redeemed from every nation through his blood.

Resolution (Revelation 6-20)

Jesus will return someday in fulfillment of the promises made to Israel to establish a literal kingdom here on earth. When he comes, "every knee will bow and every tongue will confess that Jesus Christ is Lord, to the glory of God the Father."

But it will be too late for those who failed to believe in Jesus in their lifetime. God will remove them and punish them with unbearable, eternal punishment.

He will usher those who believed in Jesus in their lifetime into his glorious kingdom. In this kingdom, there is no sin or death, no shame or strife, no pain or suffering, and no evil or unbelief. Jesus' victory over the serpent will be complete. Until that comes, those who believe in Jesus now experience foretastes of God's restoration.

Untying (Revelation 21-22)

In the end, Jesus will hand his kingdom over to God the Father, merging his kingdom with God's universal kingdom. Thus, God fulfills the promise he made long ago, restoring the earth fully as a place where his rule is honored and obeyed.

Tell me the story of Jesus

As you read this summary, and ponder its structure, you may think of other things to include in a summary of your own. One of my favorite alternatives is the hymn Fanny Crosby wrote, "Tell Me the Story of Jesus." See if you can identify the elements of story as you read the words:

> Tell me the story of Jesus,
> Write on my heart every word;
> Tell me the story most precious,
> Sweetest that ever was heard.
> Tell how the angels in chorus,
> Sang as they welcomed His birth,
> "Glory to God in the highest!
> Peace and good tidings to earth."
>
> Refrain:
> Tell me the story of Jesus,
> Write on my heart every word;
> Tell me the story most precious,
> Sweetest that ever was heard.

Fasting alone in the desert,
Tell of the days that are past,
How for our sins He was tempted,
Yet was triumphant at last.
Tell of the years of His labor,
Tell of the sorrow He bore;
He was despised and afflicted,
Homeless, rejected and poor.

Tell of the cross where they nailed Him,
Writhing in anguish and pain;
Tell of the grave where they laid Him,
Tell how He liveth again.
Love in that story so tender,
Clearer than ever I see;
Stay, let me weep while you whisper,
"Love paid the ransom for me."

Tell how He's gone back to heaven,
Up to the right hand of God:
How He is there interceding
While on this earth we must trod.
Tell of the sweet Holy Spirit
He has poured out from above;
Tell how He's coming in glory
For all the saints of his love.

Fanny J. Crosby
Public Domain

Tell more of the story

I love how Fanny Crosby's hymn shapes its telling of Jesus' larger story. But did you notice where it starts? Not with exposition, inciting incident, and rising action, but with the climax of Jesus' story. From there, it moves to the falling action and resolution. I'm not criticizing. I'm only underscoring something we need to keep in mind. Some summaries of Jesus' larger story will prove more useful than others for *story deep* analysis.

The story told in Scripture about Jesus is an epic account, full of twists and turns, revealing more and more about God as it progresses; who he is, what he values, and the way things work under his rule. It reveals more details about the rebellion and its devastating consequences. It tells more about God's judgment, and his redemption of all who believe in the Savior/Deliverer he promised. It unveils who Jesus is, what he did, and will do someday when he returns. It reveals the extent and nature of the coming restoration of all things.

When I first wrote the Gospel Story-arc summary a few years ago, I struggled with what to include and what to omit. My wife and I were serving in Asia at the time. One of our ministries was to Japanese. It didn't take long for us to figure out Japanese people did not connect spiritually or mentally to gospel presentations like the Four Spiritual Laws. We realized we had to expand our messaging and tell more of Jesus' story. But for a summary to be a summary, and not just a copy of the larger story, I had to choose which content to include, and which to exclude.

This is where story elements and story structure come into play. Take a minute to re-read the paragraph two paragraphs ago:

> The story told in Scripture about Jesus is an epic account, full of twists and turns, revealing more and more about God as it progresses; who he is, what he values, and the way things work under his rule. It reveals more details about the rebellion and its devastating consequences. It tells more about God's judgment, and his redemption of all who believe in the Savior/Deliverer he promised. It unveils who Jesus is, what he did, and will do someday when he returns. It reveals the extent and nature of the coming restoration of all things.

This paragraph is accurate in what it says. But, like Crosby's hymn, it may not provide enough information to inform the study of some Bible stories. More is needed. I've kept this in mind over the years whenever I've made minor changes to the Gospel Story-arc summary, a word here, a sentence there. I always retained the basic elements of story: character and goal; motive; antagonist; and risk and danger. I also maintained story structure. More importantly, I included enough information to meet the demands of the moment. The amount needed in one study was not the same in every study.

I wrote the Gospel Story-arc summary offered here with the same goals in mind. It contains references to the basic elements of story. It follows the story structure of a Freytag pyramid. And it contains enough to meet the demands of a *story deep* analysis. But if you need more information from the larger story to do a *story deep* analysis, add it in. Then check the story you're studying to see where it fits.

Where the Emmaus Story Fits In

Armed with the framework of the larger story about Jesus told in Scripture, it's time to discern where the story of the disciples on the road to Emmaus fits in. Doing so won't be difficult, though we'll have to be careful with what we deduce from this way of classifying the data.

The Emmaus story falls into the climax of the Bible's larger story about Jesus. Keep in mind, the climax of Jesus' story is not just his death on the cross. The climax takes in everything from Jesus' birth to his ascension and exaltation at the right hand of the Father. Just before the Ascension is where the Emmaus story fits in. The significance of this observation will become clearer, as we drill down even further to discern where our story fits into the rest of the writings of Luke, the story's author. We'll do that next.

Chapter 7

Look At Other Material from the Same Author

In chapter 3, I told the story of a book by Douglas Buckwalter that changed my life and the course of my preaching and teaching ministry. The book is *The Character and Purpose of Luke's Christology*.

In the book, Buckwalter asserts that Luke's Christology mirrored the Apostle Paul's. He bases this assertion on Luke's close association with Paul. Luke was Paul's travel companion. We know this because of the "we" passages sprinkled throughout the Book of Acts.

During those early years of the Church, various hymns and creeds circulated among Christians. The early church used them to to defend and reinforce teaching about who Jesus is and what Jesus did. A few of the hymns and creeds found their way into Paul's writings. One of them appears in Philippines 2:5-11, the so-called kenosis passage. The word kenosis comes from a verb that means to empty. Philippians 2:7 uses this word when it says that Christ Jesus emptied himself.

Buckwalter notes in his book that there are two parts to Philippians 2:5-11. The first part of the hymn asserts the humiliation of Jesus. The second, his exaltation. Buckwalter theorizes that the two parts reflect the core of Paul's Christology. He observes that since Luke was aligned with Paul, the Christ-hymn of Philippians 2:5-11 also reflected the core of Luke's Christology. From there, Buckwalter theorizes that as Luke wrote his gospel, and then the Book of Acts, he had the two-fold emphasis in mind. In the Gospel, Luke emphasized Jesus' humiliation; in the Book of Acts, his exaltation.

Buckwalter's analysis was so enlightening to me. Even now, I find it helpful in our study of the Emmaus story. Since the Emmaus story is part of the Gospel of Luke, we may find some connection to Luke's larger emphasis on the humiliation of Christ. Any connection we find will highlight the value of locating Bible stories in the larger works of their authors.

The Emmaus Story and the Rest of Luke's Gospel

First Step

There are three steps involved in locating an individual Bible story in the larger work of its author. The first and most obvious is to observe verses that surround your story. This may help you determine where a story begins and ends.

I'll share two examples.

First, the story of Elijah's appearance before Ahab in 1 Kings 17:1-7. This is where Elijah tells Ahab that "there shall be neither dew nor rain these years, except by my word." When you look at the verses both before and after, you gain valuable insight that factors into a *story deep* analysis. A look at the verses before will take you into chapter 16. There you will read just how wicked of a king Ahab was. Ahab "did evil in the sight of the Lord, more than all who were before him." Ahab's wickedness forms a predicate for Elijah's pronouncement of no dew or rain.

A look at the verses that follow 1 Kings 17:1-7 takes readers into the story of Elijah and the widow of Zarephath. The structure of the material in these verses is consistent with a betrothal type-scene. This doesn't mean that Elijah and the widow become husband and wife. They don't. But like other similar type-scenes, the one between Elijah and the widow points to something of importance that the Lord is making known. The widow says at the end, "Now I know that you are a man of God, and that the word of the Lord is in your mouth." The widow's statement reinforces something we're to know about Elijah's pronouncement to Ahab: Elijah was speaking for the Lord.

There are many other insights that come from observing the verses before and after Elijah's meeting with Ahab. I'll save these for another time. I want to move on for now to the second example.

In Acts 16:16-40, we read the story of Paul and the Philippian jailer. The inciting incident for this story appears to be Paul casting a demon out of a local slave girl. As a result, the girl's owners can no longer profit from her demonic tirades. So they become angry with Paul and have him thrown into prison. Overnight there was a great earthquake, which broke open the prison doors and freed the prisoners from their shackles. But Paul and the other prisoners did not escape. They remained in place, leading to the Philippian jailer asking Paul what he must do to be saved. Paul told him. The jailer was saved. The next day, the magistrates came and released Paul publicly.

One of the first things you'll notice about my summary is no mention of Silas, or of anyone else who was traveling with Paul and likely also thrown into prison. But I skipped a lot more than that. My focus for now is only how the verses before and after this story affect our understanding of its beginning and ending.

Since chapter 16 ends with verse 40, we have to go into Acts chapter 17 to observe verses that come after. When we do that, it's clear. The story of Paul and Philippian jailer ends with verse 40 of chapter 16.

But there are questions, story questions, raised by the ending we read in chapter 16. Why did Luke include Paul's demand for a public release from prison in the story's ending? Why also does Paul make such a big deal about his being a Roman citizen? When Paul is finally released, why doesn't he and his party leave the city right away? Who are "the brothers" he saw? Where did they come from?

When a story ending raises unanswered questions such as these, I will turn back to the story's beginning for clues. If none are there, it raises the possibility that we're looking at a scene in a story and not the story itself. What we thought was the story's beginning is the beginning of a scene.

We would have discovered this very thing in the Elijah and Ahab "story" had we scanned the surrounding verses. This discovery doesn't make scenes less interesting. But if we're going to interpret them with accuracy, we need to note what the actual story is, where it begins, and how the scene fits in.

When we look at verses that precede the scene of Paul's encounter with the slave girl, we notice the "story" of Lydia's conversion. I put the word story in quotes, because this too is only a scene. It forms a predicate for the mention of Lydia at the end. But it doesn't answer the story questions raised earlier.

Going back a little farther, we come to Acts 16:6-10 and the vision that appeared to Paul in the night: "a man of Macedonia was standing there, urging him and saying, 'Come over to Macedonia and help us.'" I believe this is where the story begins. Paul's vision of the man forms the story's inciting incident. From there to the end of chapter 16 are several scenes that lead to resolution and untying. The scene of Paul with the Philippian jailer is one of them.

I could write much more about the stories of Elijah and Ahab, and of Paul with his team in Philippi. I've only included this to make the point: looking carefully at verses that come before and after the Bible story you're analyzing is worth it. It may help you notice what you wouldn't notice otherwise. You may answer story questions that otherwise go unanswered. You may even change your mind about where your story begins and ends.

As for the Emmaus story, many will say that it begins in Luke 24:13 and ends in Luke 24:35. But when we look at verses that come before and after, it's clear that the story begins in Luke 24:1 and carries on to the end of the chapter. One reason is because without Luke 24:1-12, our story has no real inciting incident. Jesus' appearance to the disciples in verse 15 can't be it. For one, the disciples didn't recognize Jesus. For two, his appearing doesn't cause the disciples to form a new goal. They were already on their way to Emmaus.

Second Step

The second step in locating a Bible story in the larger work of its author involves connecting to the author's purpose. We take this step, realizing that not all authors state their purpose. Sometimes, we must discern it. But not in this case. Luke reveals his purpose for writing in the opening verses of Luke chapter 1:

> Inasmuch as many have undertaken to compile a narrative of the things that have been accomplished among us, just as those who from the beginning were eyewitnesses and ministers of the word have delivered them to us, it seemed good to me also, having followed all things closely for some time past, to write an orderly account for you, most excellent Theophilus, that you may have certainty concerning the things you have been taught. (Luke 1:1-4)

Knowing this purpose might help us answer one of the story questions we asked in a previous chapter. For example:

Why were the eyes of the two disciples kept from recognizing Jesus?

One thing is certain. The answer to the first question is *not* spiritual blindness. Still, the logical outline from earlier asserts:

Spiritual blindness requires divine enlightenment.

If the disciples had suffered from spiritual blindness, why didn't Luke say so? After all, his purpose was to provide a dependable account. So we should note that he says nothing about spiritual blindness. He only says that the eyes of the disciples "were kept from recognizing Jesus."

Turning the physical experience of the two disciples into a metaphor for the spiritual seems harsh. I would think that watching someone suffer and die on a cross would eliminate any expectation you might have entertained about them appearing to you alive again in a day or two. I can imagine seeing someone who looks like the person I saw dead, and thinking, *That's him!* or *That's her!* I believe I would talk myself out of that conclusion. It's a human response.

This insight may not answer the question fully. Not yet anyway. But it eliminates a wrong answer.

Third Step

The third step in locating a Bible story in the larger work of its author involves scanning the rest of the author's writings for anything that might be helpful. For example, as we scan through the Book of Acts, we find a similar ending to that of Luke's Gospel. Luke's Gospel ends with Jesus interpreting to the disciples all things concerning himself, "beginning with Moses and all the Prophets" (Luke 24:27). Jesus does this twice, as we will soon consider in more detail. The Book of Acts ends in similar fashion, but with Paul, not Jesus, "trying to convince them about Jesus from the Law of Moses and from the Prophets" (Acts 28:23). This similarity may form part of the application we make from the Emmaus story.

Scanning through the rest of the Book of Acts, or through the rest of Luke's Gospel, may also turn up the rhema that Luke intends for us to be familiar with (see the definitions in Chapter 5).

Fourth Step

The fourth step in locating a Bible story in the larger work of its author involves the story's setting. One key element of setting involves time, which breaks down into three considerations: (1) a story's location in time; (2) its duration; and (3) the time of its writing.

We know that the Emmaus story comes at the end of Luke's emphasis on Jesus' humiliation, but before Jesus' ascension to the right hand of the Father. We also know the story takes place on the day Jesus rose from the dead. For the Jews, this day was also part of the Feast of Unleavened Bread. This insight may hold the answer to another one of our questions: Why did Jesus taking bread, blessing it, breaking it, and giving it to the two disciples lead to their eyes being opened?

It turns out that the Feast of Unleavened Bread linked eating bread without leaven to two types of experience. The first was to the unpleasantness of suffering, established by association with bitter herbs (Ex. 12:8). The second was to rescue and redemption, tied to the day God brought Israel out of Egypt (Ex. 12:17). Given these meanings, did the blessing Jesus gave in front of the disciples somehow tie into both? Did it combine "This is my body..." (emphasizing suffering) and "For you will not abandon my soul to Sheol, or let your holy one see corruption" (from Psalm 16, emphasizing rescue and redemption as part of resurrection)? The element of time may provide the answer.

The duration of time factors into most Bible stories in some fashion. Some stories collapse large amounts of time, hundreds of years even, into a single statement or two. Others expand time, prompting us to slow down and inspect the details of what happened. Still others mingle the two. In the story of the two disciples to Emmaus, time slows to what happened within the hours following Jesus' resurrection from the dead. The walk from Jerusalem to Emmaus presumably takes place over 3-4 hours. Then the story pauses to the brief moments when Jesus "took the bread and blessed and broke it and gave it to them." Next, the story collapses the time it takes for the two disciples to return to Jerusalem. We're to conclude that they traveled back at night. Then time slows to spotlight the details of what happened when Jesus appears to the two and the Eleven. Time then jumps ahead 40 days to focus on Jesus' ascension. Then it summarizes what happened as the disciples waited for Pentecost. Each of these features of the duration of time is worth pondering, but for now, I will only note them.

Finally, the time of Luke's writing. Luke wrote his Gospel and the Book of Acts many years after the events he chronicled. He did this to assure Theophilus of the accuracy of the things he had been taught. This element of time may help us answer one other story question from our list: How does this story apply to life now?

You may recall that the creator of the logical outline on Bibleoutlines.com offered these applications:

Spiritual blindness requires divine enlightenment

Only Jesus can resolve our spiritual confusion and despair

We must listen in faith to the exposition of Jesus in the Scriptures

Divine enlightenment—The opening of our eyes to see Jesus—confirms the resurrection

The time of Luke's writing calls the last three into question. Luke wrote many years after Jesus ascended. So by the time of his writing, it was no longer possible for someone to encounter Jesus physically. That means no longer being able to "listen in faith" or to "see Jesus." If Jesus were to resolve our spiritual confusion and despair, he would have to do it in some fashion other than with his physical presence.

Luke wrote the story to assure Theophilus of the accuracy of the things he had been taught. By implication, this purpose includes guiding Theophilus in how he should apply these things to his life. So was Luke trying to frustrate Theophilus, calling on him to see and listen to Jesus when he knew that was no longer possible? Was he expecting him to think that "seeing" Jesus now doesn't mean "seeing" him, but only believing in him? Or that "listening" to Jesus now doesn't mean "listening" to him, but to his word mediated through others? Perhaps, but I think we all agree: there is a substantial difference between actually seeing and listening to Jesus versus not. Jesus himself distinguished between the two in his response to Thomas in John 20:29:

> "Have you believed because you have seen me? Blessed are those who have not seen and yet have believed."

In the end, the timing of Luke's writing, tied to his purpose, suggests there's more to the applications Luke has in mind for Theophilus, and for people like us.

Chapter 8

Create a Step Outline

I've written a lot so far about the downside of using outlines to analyze Bible stories. But I've always referred to these outlines as *logical*. These are the kind outlines we call Roman numeral outlines. Some writing apps call them Harvard style outlines. Whatever the name, I've been harping against these types of outlines for several chapters. I've been saying they are the wrong tool to do *story deep* analysis. As mentioned earlier, Traina and Bauer stipulate their use at the end of an analytical process. The problem is, past training prompts us to use logical outlines when we begin our studies. This means using them to analyze Bible content, not to summarize and report on our investigation.

In this chapter, I'm going to write about a different type of outline, one that's called a *step outline*. Step outlines play a part near the start of a *story deep* analysis of Bible stories. Creating them allows you to sharpen or expand the observations you make early on. They also allow you to classify data more thoughtfully. This may allow you to make high-quality deductions and spur you on to more accurate results. By the end of the process, step outlines may even smooth the way through verification.

More About Story Structure

Before I show how to create a step outline for the Emmaus story, I need to share more about story structure. Besides the Freytag pyramid, I have observed three other types of structures that appear to organize the *story-arcs* of Bible stories. I put the word *appear* in italics for two reasons. First, it's possible that further study would change my understanding of the structures I'm going to list. Second, it's also possible that the ancients used story structures not on my list.

Some contend that modern story structures impose on structures the ancients used. And they may be right. But this doesn't make moderns 100% wrong. Most people recognize there is something universal about storytelling, going back as far into history as we can. Take, for example, the first story ever told by a human being (that we know about)—the tale Adam spun to excuse his disobedience in the Garden:

> The Lord God called out to the man and said to him, "Where are you?"

> And he said, "I heard the sound of you in the garden and I was afraid, because I was naked, and I hid myself."

> He said, "Who told you that you were naked? Have you eaten of the tree I commanded you not to eat?"

> The man said, "The woman you gave to be with me, she gave me fruit of the tree, and I ate."

(Genesis 3:9-12)

This exchange between God and Adam forms part of a larger story the Bible tells us about the Fall. But that's not why I've labeled it as the first story ever told. It's not just a story about what happened near when time began; my point is the rhetorical strategy Adam used to answer God's query. Adam answered with a story about himself: he is the main character; his goal was to hide himself from God; his motive was fear; the antagonist was the woman God gave to him.

I believe Adam used a story to answer God because of the way God programmed his mind. God programmed Adam's and everyone else's mind to process our experiences through story. Scientists have confirmed this through the wonder of fMRI (functional magnetic resonance imaging). Their findings show what our brains do with sensory inputs. Our brains take the inputs and organize them into story categories. Even infants as young as ten months old have been shown to process the information they take in using the story elements of goal and motive. This happens on a subconscious level.

So, sure, it's possible the ancients crafted their stories with structures different from those we use. But that doesn't make their structures unknowable, or so different from ours that our only recourse is to analyze content with logical outlines.

With these caveats, here is my list of story-structure types, including the Freytag pyramid:

Freytag pyramid

Type-scene

Dialogue-event

The McKee eight

Freytag Pyramid

The first type of story structure on the list is Freytag pyramid. Since I have already reviewed the structure of a Freytag pyramid, I won't repeat it here. Besides, I do not believe a Freytag Pyramid is the most useful structure for analyzing the Emmaus story, as I will soon explain.

Type-scene

The second story structure on the list is type-scene. This kind of structure is a patterned way of arranging story elements. I mentioned this type of structure in the previous chapter. I wrote that Elijah's encounter with the widow of Zarephath follows the pattern of a betrothal type-scene. Hebrew scholar Robert Alter explains the pattern:

> The betrothal type-scene, then, must take place with the future bridegroom, or his surrogate, having journeyed to a foreign land. There he encounters a girl... or girls at a well. Someone, either the man or the girl, then draws water from the well; afterward, the girl or girls rush to bring home the news of the stranger's arrival (the verbs "hurry" and "run" are given recurrent emphasis at this junction of the type-scene); finally, a betrothal is concluded between the stranger and the girl, in the majority of instances, only after he has been invited to a meal.

Alter, Robert. The Art of Biblical Narrative (p. 62). Basic Books. Kindle Edition.

(Alter admits that we do not possess direct knowledge of the actual conventions Bible writers used to craft their stories. This positions us as having to discern patterns, not unlike what we're doing now in our study of the Emmaus story.)

The pattern of a type-scene calls for, but doesn't require, conformity in all of its parts. In Genesis 24, the story of Abraham's servant and his search for a wife for Isaac conforms to the pattern in nearly every way. The story of Elijah and the widow does not. Neither does the story of Jesus and the Samaritan woman, which also seems to follow the pattern. These latter two stories show a betrothal type-scene does not have to end in marriage.

In one sense, a betrothal type scene in the Bible is like the typical pattern of a modern-day love story. Not that all betrothal type-scenes are about love; they're not. I make the comparison, because the structure of modern-day love stories, especially when they're told through film, is so well-known that people expect them to contain certain elements.

For example, somewhere near the end of the story, the two lovers kiss. Then the story ends. Imagine how frustrating it would be if the two lovers did not kiss. Or if the movie didn't include any conflict that almost ends their relationship. Most people would walk away disappointed. They'd call the movie *boring*, or something worse. That's because our intuition leads us to notice changes in the elements that we expect to see in some types of story. When the expected elements go missing, or are substantially changed, our minds search for an explanation. Is it because the storyteller lacks talent? Or were the changes intentional? If so, what's the significance?

Dialogue Event

The third type of story structure is a dialogue event. This type of structure often contains narration. But its chief feature is a pattern of direct speech involving a character in dialogue with someone; perhaps God, perhaps others, perhaps himself. Keep in mind the word dialogue does not mean talk between two people. It means *through speech*. Dialogue is the means through which the characters in a story express the actions they take toward, or expect from, others. Thus, through direct speech, characters act and react, and move a story forward.

Herein lies one of the most important keys to story deep analysis:

> **Even if you pay attention to nothing else about story structure, pay attention to the patterns of action/reaction. There often are many treasures of meaning hidden in these patterns.**

A premier example of a dialogue event story structure is the account of Noah and the Flood in Genesis 6-9. Until the very end of the story in chapter 9, God is the only one who speaks. But he isn't the only one in the story who acts and reacts. Here is the pattern: God speaks/acts, followed by Noah not speaking/yet acting. Keep in mind that not speaking isn't the same as not acting/not reacting. Whenever God speaks, Noah reacts with obedience.

The pattern breaks at the end of Chapter 8, and a new pattern begins. This new pattern begins with Noah acting, followed by God speaking/acting. God blesses Noah and spells out the conditions of the covenant of chapter 9. This new pattern continues to the end of chapter 9. Once again, Noah acts, this time through direct speech. Though God and Noah's sons say nothing in reply, both react in their own way to Noah's blessing and cursing on his sons: God by fulling Noah's words; the descendants of Ham by rebelling against them.

The McKee Eight

The fourth type of story structure is what I call the McKee eight. Robert McKee is a world famous, world-class story expert and has trained thousands of people in story craft. McKee advocates for story structure based on eight stages, with each stage operating according to a prime principle. Here is a brief explanation:

Target audience/Meaningful emotional effect

Well-crafted stories are not just endless cycles of this happened, then this happened, then this happened, then.... Instead, they are commentaries on the values of life and relationships. As stories unfold, the positive or negative charges tied to these values change. The changes create an emotional experience of pain or pleasure. The goal of a well-crafted story is to tie these emotions to the story's moral argument (a view on how the world works or should work). This results in a meaningful emotional effect on the audience.

Subject matter/Balance

The subject matter of a story includes its physical and social setting; its characters; and its core value. The core value of story is expressed as a binary. For example, the core value of a story isn't love; it's love/hate. It isn't justice; it's justice/injustice. It isn't joy; it's joy/sorrow. As a story begins, the story's core value carries a neutral "charge", meaning it appears to be in balance in the life of the main character.

Inciting incident/Imbalance

Something happens that upsets the balance of the core value in the life of the main character.

Object of desire/Unfulfilled need

In response, the main character believes there is something he or she must have to regain control and restore balance. This is the main character's object of desire or goal. The object of desire may be physical, psychological, or spiritual. Or some combination of the three.

First action/Tactical choice

The main character's object of desire demands that he or she take action to get it.

First reaction/Violation of expectation

However, there are forces in the world that do not respond as expected. Instead, they block the main character, often moving him or her farther away from the object of desire.

Crisis choice/Insight

A crisis choice is the action a character chooses in the climax to achieve his/her goal. If successful, the character's choice restores balance to life. Along the way, the emotional charge of the story's core value changes. The changes can feel slight or overwhelming. They can range from negative to positive, and back again.

Climatic reaction/Closure

A meaningful emotional effect accompanies the main character finally getting his or her object of desire.

This summary of the McKee Eight doesn't do justice to the depth of McKee's understanding of story. Still, it will prove to be a helpful guide for our *story deep* analysis of the Emmaus story. For one, it will provide a framework to insert our observations about character, goal, motive, antagonist, risk, and danger. It will also help us make sense of the order of events in our story. But perhaps its most useful help will come from its nudging us to create a step outline as our next task.

Plugging the Emmaus story into the McKee eight

Target audience/meaningful emotional effect

There's not much to add under this heading just yet. We don't yet know the story's meaningful emotional effect. And our understanding of it may affect our understanding of who the target audience is. Besides, using the McKee eight is not a linear process. In our case, "subject matter/balance" feels like a better place to start.

Subject matter/Balance

It's clear from Luke 24:13 that the main characters of the Emmaus story are the two disciples. The two were among those whom Mary Magdalene, Joanna, and Mary, the mother of Jesus, told of their experience at Jesus' tomb (see 24:9). It's also clear that the two are on their way from Jerusalem to the village of Emmaus, about seven miles away. But there's no feel just yet for what the story's core binary value is.

Inciting Incident/Imbalance

The inciting incident appears to take place at 24:15, when Jesus draws near the two disciples and starts walking with them. The text adds in 24:16, "But their eyes were kept from recognizing him." This could be a hint of the story's core value. Is it not recognizing/recognizing the resurrected Jesus?

But remember, I said that filling in the McKee Eight isn't a linear process.

So, as soon as we ask, we realize our initial guess doesn't fit. Not recognizing/recognizing Jesus wasn't on minds of the two disciples when Jesus first joined them on the road. They were pondering what happened back in Jerusalem. This includes no one having seen Jesus alive after the crucifixion.

But seeing/not seeing Jesus can't be the core binary value. Jesus did not throw the lives of the two disciples out of balance when he joined them on their walk. How could he? They didn't recognize him.

The bottom line—Jesus' joining the disciples on their walk seems like it could be the story's inciting incident. But I'm still not sure of the story's core value.

Object of Desire/Unfulfilled Need

Things don't get better as we move on to the object of desire/unfulfilled need. If the inciting incident is Jesus joining the disciples on the road, what object of desire does that create? It can't be to see Jesus alive. The disciples already desired this.

I realize I'm struggling here. I have little to say about the target audience and meaningful emotional effect. I can't identify the subject matter and core binary value. And I'm unsure of the inciting incident. So what did I learn from the McKee

Eight? I learned the power of creating a step-outline before using the McKee eight or any other structure to classify story content.

A step outline

I'll return to the McKee Eight in time. But first, I'll walk through creating a step-outline. A step-outline summarizes what happens in a story step-by-step. It's not written with Roman numerals, alliteration, or parallelism. It features action verbs embedded in complete sentences. Here's what that looks like for the story of the two disciples on their way to Emmaus:

Two disciples begin walking the seven miles or so from Jerusalem to Emmaus on the day after Jesus appeared to certain women, on the day he rose from the dead.

The two talk with each other about what had happened.

Jesus joins the two. [The two disciples' eyes are kept from recognizing Jesus.]

The two disciples say and do nothing at all in response to Jesus joining them.

So Jesus asks the two disciples to tell him what they were talking about.

The two disciples ask Jesus if he is the only visitor to Jerusalem who does not know these things.

Jesus asks, "What things?"

The disciples explain their disappointment over what happened in Jerusalem, Jesus crucified by the chief priests and rulers, the report of the women's visit to Jesus' tomb, the others going and finding the tomb like the women said, but no one saw Jesus, and now it's the third day.

Jesus calls the disciples "fools," and "slow of heart," and asks, "Was it not necessary that the Christ should suffer these things and enter into his glory?"

The disciples say nothing.

Jesus tells all things in the Scriptures concerning himself, beginning with Moses and then all the Prophets.

The disciples draw near to Emmaus.

Jesus acts as though he is going on.

The disciples urge Jesus to stay with them on a pretense.

Jesus stays with them.

The disciples share a meal with Jesus.

Jesus takes the bread and blesses and breaks it, and gives it to the disciples.

The two disciples' eyes are opened and they recognize Jesus.

Jesus vanishes from their sight.

The disciples reflect on what just happened and return to Jerusalem to tell the eleven.

As they are talking, Jesus appears among them and greets them.

The two disciples and the eleven are startled and afraid.

Jesus asks them why they are troubled and doubting, then offers proof of his identity and bodily resurrection

The disciples marvel but still don't totally believe.

Jesus asks them for something to eat.

The disciples give Jesus a piece of broiled fish.

Jesus eats it in front of them.

Jesus reminds the two and the eleven of things he had told them before his death. He opens their minds to understand his story from the Scriptures.

Jesus tells the disciples they are witnesses of these things and repeats his promise to clothe them with power from on high.

Jesus leads the disciples out to Bethany, blesses them, and ascends into heaven.

The two disciples and the eleven worship Jesus, then return to Jerusalem with great joy to wait to be clothed with power from on high. Meanwhile, they are continually in the temple blessing God.

I recommend that you re-read the text of the Emmaus story included in Chapter 1. Then browse through the step outline one more time. You will see the goal is to lay out what happened using present tense, active verbs, without interpreting what happened.

Now that we have our step-outline in hand, we still won't return to the McKee Eight. Not just yet. First, we'll need to treat this outline. More about that next.

Chapter 9

Treat the Step Outline

I n the previous chapter, I created a step-outline describing what happened step-by-step in the Emmaus story. I did this to look for patterns of action/reaction that align with the framework of the McKee eight. In this chapter, our aim is to leverage the explanatory power of the patterns we observe. Doing this will require us to treat the step-outline.

To treat a step-outline, we must identify the subtext of each action/reaction. This involves using a gerund to describe each action/reaction of a story's characters. Gerunds are verb forms that function as nouns. In English, gerunds take the -ing form of a verb. The gerunds you choose to treat your step-outline won't be the -ing form of the verbs the story uses to describe what a character says or does. Those are the verbs you used to create the step-outline. Treating the step-outline means choosing other verbs, ones meant to describe the subtext of what happened.

For example, this is the first entry in the step-outline I created for the Emmaus story:

> Two disciples begin walking the seven miles or from Jerusalem to Emmaus on the day after Jesus appeared to certain women, on the day he rose from the dead.

In treating this, I won't reuse the verb walking, because walking is what the disciples were doing in the story. Instead, I will try to discern what their walking from Jerusalem to Emmaus tells me about their motives or state of mind. Here is what this looks like:

The two disciples' *giving up* on the redemption of Israel through Jesus

This is my best assessment of the two disciples' motive and state of mind as they set out for Emmaus. The story itself led me to this assessment. In Luke 24:19-24, the two disciples connect their profound disappointment over Jesus' not rising from the dead to the dashing of their hope that he was the one to redeem Israel. Since Jesus was expected to rise and appear in Jerusalem, the two disciples' leaving Jerusalem meant they had given up on Jesus being resurrected. Which also meant giving up on the redemption of Israel through Jesus.

My thought process here underscores something about using the *story deep* method that I highlighted at the beginning:

> The process I'm sharing is not linear, but more back-and-forth.
> The actual process of studying Bible stories as story may take you
> back and forth from room to room more than once.

Here's another way to say the same thing: As we study Bible stories as story, we're never expected to act like we don't know what we know. So the process itself does not, and should not, require that I put out of mind what I know from other parts of the story. Therefore, taking in what I know from the story about the two disciples and their disappointment, disappointment the story itself reveals to me, I posit my treatment of their leaving Jerusalem for Emmaus. Once again:

The two disciples' *giving up* on the redemption of Israel through Jesus

The rest of my treatment appears below. Notice the format I follow. I indented and bold-faced each treatment statement below its corresponding entry from the step-outline. I also italicized the gerunds to make them easier to spot:

Two disciples begin walking the seven miles or from Jerusalem to

Emmaus on the day after Jesus appeared to certain women, on the day he rose from the dead.

The two disciples *giving up* on the redemption of Israel through Jesus

The two talk with each other about what had happened.

The two *processing* their miscalculation and disappointment

Jesus joins the two. [The two disciples' eyes are kept from recognizing Jesus.]

Jesus *inserting* himself in the conversation

The two disciples say and do nothing at all in response to Jesus joining them.

The two disciples *hoping* that Jesus would give them a chance to talk about something else

So Jesus asks the two disciples to tell him what they were talking about.

Jesus *forcing* them to stay on topic

The two disciples ask Jesus if he is the only visitor to Jerusalem who does not know these things.

The two disciples *insulting* Jesus

Jesus asks, "What things?"

Jesus *ignoring* the insult

The disciples explain their disappointment over what happened in Jerusalem, Jesus crucified by the chief priests and rulers, the report of the women's visit to Jesus' tomb, the others going and finding the tomb like the women said, but no one saw Jesus, and now it's the third day.

The two disciples *looking* for sympathy

Jesus calls the disciples "fools," and "slow of heart," and asks, "Was it not necessary that the Christ should suffer these things and enter into his glory?"

Jesus *insulting* the two disciples

The disciples say nothing.

The two disciples *absorbing* the insult

Jesus tells all things in the Scriptures concerning himself, beginning with Moses and then all the Prophets.

Jesus *redirecting* their thoughts to his story

The disciples draw near to Emmaus.

The two disciples *clinging* to their (original, outward) goal

Jesus acts as though he is going on.

Jesus *feigning*

The disciples urge Jesus to stay with them on a pretense.

The two disciples *feigning*

Jesus stays with them.

Jesus *welcoming* opportunity

The disciples share a meal with Jesus.

The disciples *welcoming* Jesus

Jesus takes the bread and blesses and breaks it, and gives it to the disciples.

Jesus *revealing* himself

The two disciples' eyes are opened and they recognize Jesus.

The two disciples *recognizing* Jesus

Jesus vanishes from their sight.

Jesus *prompting* the two disciples' return to Jerusalem

The disciples reflect on what just happened and return to Jerusalem to tell the eleven.

The two disciples *processing* the new information

As they are talking, Jesus appears among them and greets them.

Jesus *validating* the report of the two disciples

The two disciples and the eleven are startled and afraid.

The disciples *denying* their own eyes

Jesus asks them why they are troubled and doubting, then offers proof of his identity and bodily resurrection

Jesus offering *proof*

The disciples marvel but still don't totally believe.

The disciples still *doubting*

Jesus asks them for something to eat.

Jesus *offering* more proof

The disciples give Jesus a piece of broiled fish.

The disciples *cooperating* with Jesus

Jesus eats it in front of them.

Jesus *showing* he isn't a ghost

Jesus reminds the two and the eleven of things he had previously told them. He opens their minds to understand his story from the Scriptures.

Jesus *reinforcing* the foundational importance of his larger story

Jesus tells the disciples they are witnesses of these things and repeats his promise to clothe them with power from on high.

Jesus *commissioning* the two and the eleven

Jesus leads the disciples out to Bethany, blesses them, and ascends into heaven.

Jesus *allowing* the disciples to witness his ascension

The two disciples and the eleven worship Jesus, then return to Jerusalem with great joy to wait to be clothed with power from on high. Meanwhile, they are continually in the temple blessing God.

The disciples *accepting* their commission

When you're finished treating your step-outline, you can go back and make changes if you wish. You can change which gerund you use to characterize an action/reaction. Or you can adjust the wording of some other part of your step-outline. What matters is that you're using a story deep process to further classify all the data you've collected so far. These data include: what you observed in the story, and from the story's connections to the larger story about Jesus. Or from the larger work of the story's author. Or from any other background information you may have uncovered so far. Again, what matters is that you're using a process matched to the genre of story, a *story deep* process.

All this work has prepared us now to return to the McKee eight. We'll do that next.

Chapter 10

Treat the Story's Structure

T reating the story's structure means taking the insights we've gained from the data we've collected and classified so far and plugging them into the McKee eight. The goal is to discover how, and even whether, what we think about the story makes sense and coheres.

Keep in mind, the process of treating the story's structure, like the process we're using overall, does not have to be linear. With the Emmaus story, we've already made a couple of attempts to analyze story structure in a linear fashion. On both occasions, we got stuck. So I will begin this time by analyzing how the story ends, hoping this yields further insight into the story's binary core value. If I can discern the story's core binary value, I'll be able to go back to the beginning of the McKee eight structure and work my way from there.

Here is how I treated the step-outline's ending of the Emmaus story:

> Jesus tells the disciples they are witnesses of these things and repeats his promise to clothe them with power from on high.

Jesus *commissioning* the two and the eleven

Jesus leads the disciples out to Bethany, blesses them, and ascends into heaven.

Jesus *allowing* the disciples to see witness his ascension

The two disciples and the eleven worship Jesus, then return to Jerusalem with great joy to wait to be clothed with power from on high. Meanwhile, they are continually in the temple blessing God.

The two disciples and the eleven *accepting* their commission

What can we make of this ending? Do the two disciples and the eleven accept their commission because they saw Jesus, and for no other reason? If so, we should confirm not seeing/seeing Jesus resurrected as the story's core binary value. But then we still need to figure out the inciting incident. Remember, the inciting incident changes the charge of the story's core binary value. This change leads to the formation of the main character's goal. Which leaves us with a dilemma. When did our characters ever not want to see the resurrected Jesus?

Our characters wanted to see Jesus from the beginning. They even told Jesus how disappointed they were that others in their company had not seen him:

> "Some of those who were with us went to the tomb and found it just as the women said, but him they did not see." (Luke 24:24)

There must be some other core binary value in play. The value of not seeing/seeing Jesus resurrected doesn't fit other parts of the story's structure. The value never changes its charge. Nor does it point to a viable inciting incident.

Back to the question: What exactly was it that led the two disciples and the eleven to accept their commissioning from Jesus? Could it be that they could finally make sense of everything that happened to Jesus at the hands of the chief priests and rulers? That the Scripture's larger story about Jesus was still in play? Stated more simply, could the core binary value of the Emmaus story be dissonance/consonance?

The charge of such a value changes dramatically after the women and others report on their visit to the tomb. They saw angels, but not Jesus. The two disciples explain their confusion:

> Concerning Jesus of Nazareth, a man who was a prophet mighty in deed and word before God and all the people, and how our chief priests and rulers delivered him up to be condemned to death, and crucified him. But we had hoped he was the one to redeem Israel. Yes, and besides all this, it is now the third day since these things happened. Moreover, some women of our company amazed us. They were at the tomb early in the morning, and when they did not find his body, they came back saying that they had seen a vision of angels who said that he was alive. Some of those who were with us went to the tomb and found it just as the women had said, but him they did not see. (Luke 24:19-24)

The two disciples described a roller coaster of cognitive dissonance. They had hoped that Jesus was the one to redeem Israel. But that didn't happen. Jesus died on the cross instead. The two disciples then turned to the promise of resurrection, their hopes raised by the amazing reports of the women who visited the tomb. But the women didn't see Jesus. How could the two keep on believing and hoping when every stitch of real world evidence before them screamed they were wrong?

So while the story flashes back to the inciting incident part way through, the inciting incident itself takes place prior to the start of our story. When it does, it changes the charge of the core binary value decidedly to the negative. And that's how our story begins, with the two disciples heading toward Emmaus. They set their sights on Emmaus to restore the dissonance/consonance balance of their lives.

After I first posited this in my study of the Emmaus story, I began searching online for more information on cognitive dissonance. One book I found is, "When Prophecy Fails." Listed among the book's authors is Leon Festinger, a widely recognized expert on the subject. So the book has added to my insight.

Story Scenes and Beats

I feel much more at ease now with adding detail to the McKee Eight. But before I do, I want to say a word about story scenes and beats. Scenes in stories are crafted around turning points, which are changes in the charge of value, possibly the story's core binary value, or some other value that matters. A story beat is a unit of action/reaction that combines with other beats to form a scene.

The Emmaus story contains four scenes:

(1) On the road on the way to Emmaus

(2) At Emmaus

(3) Back in Jerusalem with the eleven

(4) Jesus' ascension at Bethany and the disciples back in Jerusalem

Notice that scene 4 takes place in two locations. The possibility of a scene taking place in two locations illustrates something worth pointing out. Scenes are not primarily about shifts in time and place, but about turning points.

Adding detail to the McKee eight

Scene 1 - On the Road to Emmaus

Subject Matter/Balance

The main characters of the story are two disciples. Luke 24:13 says the "two of them," the words of them further identifying the two as among "all the rest" mentioned in Luke 24:9. The two are among those whom Mary Magdalene, Joanna, and Mary, the mother of Jesus, told of their experience at Jesus' tomb. The two are on their way from Jerusalem to the village of Emmaus, about seven miles away.

The subject matter of the story is dissonance/consonance, which begins out of balance.

Inciting Incident/Imbalance

The inciting incident takes place before our story begins. The story refers to it in a flashback (Luke 24:19-24). The two disciples watched Jesus suffer and die at the hands of the chief priests and rulers. They also learned that none of the women or any of the others had seen Jesus alive. The change in the charge of the story's core value moves decidedly to the negative at the opening.

Object of Desire/Unfulfilled Need:

Because of the decidedly negative charge of the story's core value, an object of desire forms in the minds of the two disciples. They decide to head for Emmaus.

Reaching Emmaus was both their goal and their first tactical choice.

It was their goal in that the two clearly headed there. But they decided based on a deeper, inner goal. The two disciples wanted to restore consonance in their lives. For now, the destination of Emmaus represented their success.

Characters almost always have both outward goals and inward goals. They rarely connect the two until later in a story.

Beat 1

Action/Tactical Choice

The first tactical choice of the two disciples was to make their way to Emmaus. Getting to Emmaus, they believed, would help them overcome their dissonance.

Festinger and the others list only three ways to overcome the dissonance. The first is to reinterpret what happened. The second is to acquire new information. The third is to abandon altogether whatever belief is at stake. All three ways also require help from the social system of the victim.

In our story, the two disciples leave Jerusalem for Emmaus deeply wounded. In their minds, their deeply held beliefs about Jesus were dis-confirmed. Emmaus represents a fresh start, a place where they could make sense of what happened and recover psychologically.

In the step-outline, I describe the two as "giving up on the redemption of Israel through Jesus." The story says as much later on. If the two hadn't given up, they would have remained in Jerusalem and kept on expecting Jesus to appear and fulfill Israel's redemption. So leaving Jerusalem meant they had given up in their disappointment.

Reaction

The disciples might have hoped for a private long walk to Emmaus to sort things out in their minds. Though the two disciples had begun to accept a different reality, their disappointment was still there, as was the shame they felt over having been so wrong. So the two try to process their miscalculation and disappointment by talking it out. But only with each other.

Then Jesus joins them and inserts himself into their conversation. The text adds in 24:16, "But their eyes were kept from recognizing him."

Beat 2

Action/Tactical Choice

Kept from recognizing Jesus, the disciples say nothing at first. Perhaps they weren't confident Jesus would understand. Perhaps they were hoping he would keep to himself, or at least give them a chance to talk about something else. Either way, the two disciples weren't ready to bring Jesus in.

Reaction

But Jesus forces them to stay on topic, asking, "What is this conversation that you are holding with each other as you walk?"

Jesus' question is the equivalent of ripping a bandage from a fresh wound. It would be impossible to bring him in without the two disciples re-living their disappointment and shame.

The charge of the story's core binary value of dissonance/consonance turns decidedly to the negative.

The original goal of the two disciples takes a back seat as their inner goal expresses itself differently. Perhaps the two disciples even realize that there is more to their intentions than just the outward goal of getting to Emmaus. Regardless, a new object of desire forms in their minds. The two now need to persuade Jesus that they are rational actors. They want him to know they are undeserving of any negative sentiment directed toward them for the position they're in now. On a deeper level, the two also feel the need to persuade themselves of the same. Deeper still, the two must restore consonance in their lives.

Beat 3

Action/Tactical choice

The two disciples insult Jesus, asking if he is the only visitor to Jerusalem who does not know these things.

It may seem odd at first to insult someone whom you're trying to win over to your way of thinking. But keep in mind, the desire to persuade Jesus of their rationality is the disciples' conscious desire, a desire they would have been self-aware of. They may not have been as aware of their even deeper desire to persuade themselves of their rationality.

Often, it is our subconscious, deeper level desires that motivate our actions. By insulting the stranger's awareness, the two disciples cushion the possibility for themselves that the stranger might not see things their way— *"After all, he doesn't seem to know what happened. He for sure knows much less than we know. Why should we care what he thinks?"*

The disciples' insult also signals that the stranger should be open to their interpretation of the facts— *"We know a lot more than you, so you should see these things our way."*

Reaction

Jesus ignores the insult and asks, "What things?"
The charge of the story's core binary value of dissonance/consonance turns slightly back to the positive.

Beat 4

Action/Tactical Choice

The two disciples look for sympathy. They try to bring Jesus on their side by plowing through the details of their disappointment over what happened in Jerusalem:

Jesus crucified by the chief priests and rulers, the report of the women's visit to Jesus' tomb, the others going and finding the tomb like the women said, but no one seeing Jesus, and now it's the third day, dashing their hopes that Jesus was the One to redeem Israel.

Reaction

Jesus insults the two disciples, calling them "fools," and "slow of heart." Jesus asks, "Was it not necessary that the Christ should suffer these things and enter into his glory?"

The charge of the story's core binary value of dissonance/consonance turns doubly negative.

Beat 5

Action/Tactical Choice

The two disciples say nothing and absorb the insult.

Reaction

Jesus redirects the minds of the two disciples to his story. He tells them all things in the Scriptures concerning himself, beginning with Moses and then all the Prophets.

The charge of the story's core binary value of dissonance/consonance turns positive.

Scene 2 - Somewhere Near Emmaus

Beat 1

Action/Tactical choice

The two disciples cling to their outward goal and draw near to Emmaus.

Two hundred years or so earlier, Emmaus was the site of a famous battle between two very different kinds of soldiers. The first was highly trained and well-equipped. The second, not so much. The soldiers were led by two very different kinds of men. The first was led by a general from the army of Antiochus Epiphanes. The second by Judah Maccabee.

Antiochus' general based his troops in Emmaus to support a corrupt high priest in Jerusalem. But things didn't go well. He and his army suffered a humiliating defeat. The battle became well known. So did Judah Maccabee and his rag-tag group of volunteers. And so did Emmaus.

For the two disciples, Emmaus symbolized the triumph of ordinary Jews and their Messiah over a corrupt political and religious establishment. Walking there symbolized for them a return to the consonance of their hoping for God's redemption for Israel.

Ironically, the text says that the two disciples and Jesus drew near to Emmaus, not arrived in Emmaus. The two were so close to achieving their outward goal. But it was a goal that could never deliver. The two disciples achieve their desire instead in a way that exceeds their expectations.

Reaction - Jesus reveals himself

This fourth reaction consists of four beats. Notice the story reverses the pattern of the first scene, with Jesus now acting, the two disciples the reacting:

Beat 2

Action - Jesus feigns his going on.

Reaction - The two disciples feign concern for Jesus' well-being to mask their desire to hear more. They ask Jesus to stay with them.

Beat 3

Action - Jesus welcomes the opportunity and stays with the disciples.

Reaction - The disciples welcome Jesus and share a meal with him.

Beat 4

Action - Jesus reveals himself through his taking the bread, blessing it, breaking it, and giving to the disciples.

Reaction - The eyes of two disciples are opened and they recognize Jesus.

Beat 5

Action - Jesus vanishes from their sight, prompting the two disciples to return to Jerusalem to tell the eleven.

Reaction - The two disciples process what just happened and return to Jerusalem to tell the others.

The charge of the story's core binary value of dissonance/consonance turns doubly positive.

Scene 3 - The Two Disciples in Jerusalem with the Eleven.

Beat 1

Action/tactical choice - The two disciples tell the eleven what happened.

Reaction - Jesus validates the report of the two disciples.

Beat 2

Action/tactical choice - Jesus appears to the two together with the eleven

Reaction - The two disciples and the eleven deny their own eyes, becoming startled and afraid, and think they saw a ghost.

Beat 3

Action/tactical choice - Jesus mildly chastises them, offers proof his identity and bodily resurrection.

Reaction - The two disciples and the eleven accept Jesus' offer, but still doubt.

Beat 4

Action/tactical choice - Jesus asks for something to eat.

Reaction - The group gives Jesus a piece of broiled fish.

Beat 5

Action/tactical choice: Jesus eats it before them.

Reaction: The two and the eleven stop doubting

Beat 6

Action/tactical choice - Jesus reminds the two and the eleven of things he told them before, opening their minds to understand his story from Scripture, calling them witnesses of these things, and repeating his promise to clothe them with power from on high.

Reaction - The disciples' faith response (implied).

This scene features doubt/faith as a second binary value. By the end of the scene, the value of doubt/faith changes its charge doubly to the positive.

The charge of the core binary value of dissonance/consonance also changes doubly to the positive.

Scene 4 - at Bethany

Action/tactical choice - Jesus leads the group to Bethany, blesses them, and ascends into heaven.

Reaction - The disciples accept their commission. They worship Jesus, then return to Jerusalem with great joy to wait to be clothed with power from on high. Meanwhile, they are continually in the temple blessing God.

The charge of the story's core binary value of dissonance/consonance turns doubly positive and is infused with emotions of joy, gratitude, and purpose.

Chapter 11

Summarize and Answer Questions

W e've come a long way already in our story deep analysis of the Emmaus story. We started with reading the story. Then we asked story questions. Next, we looked for any story elements that stood out. Then we discerned where the story might fit in the Bible's larger story about Jesus and in the rest of Luke's writings. From there, we looked at the inductive process and whether logical outlines are the right tool for a story deep analysis. When the answer was "No," we continued our analysis using a step-outline. We found that step-outlines are more suited for analyzing stories. Then we treated our step-outline, and the story structure after that. Now we're here, ready to summarize what we've uncovered so far in our study.

If I were to plug all we've done so far into the acres of diamonds metaphor, I would say that the Emmaus story has been like a field rumored to contain many precious gems of various sizes. We're certain the gems are there, but they're buried in various places in the field and hidden from sight. So first we stake our claim. The field is ours to mine. Then we select the proper tools. Then we dig, gathering the gems we uncover. We sort them. We inspect them. And we marvel at their beauty.

Where we are now is analogous to gathering, sorting, and inspecting the gems.

We'll begin with Emmaus story elements and structure. Then we'll answer the story questions we posed at the beginning.

Emmaus Story Elements

Main character(s)

The two disciples; one of them named Cleopas; the other unnamed.

Their Goal or Object of Desire

The outward goal of the two disciples was to reach the village of Emmaus. Their inward goal was to restore consonance.

Motive

The two disciples were seeking to restore consonance in their lives. They saw Jesus suffer and die on the cross. But they did not see him resurrected. As far as they knew, the corrupt political and religious leaders had triumphed. Staying in Jerusalem would only remind them of their disappointment and of how wrong they were. They believed they had to make a complete break from Jerusalem to restore consonance.

Antagonist

There are two antagonists. The first is Jesus. Jesus' appearance on the road, along with the questions he asked, block the disciples' progress toward both of their goals. The second is the two disciples themselves. The two mistakenly believe that traveling to Emmaus will resolve their dissonance. If they got out of Jerusalem, there wouldn't be so much to remind them of how wrong they were. But their leaving cut them off from the better strategy of acquiring new information.

Risk

The two disciples blamed their dissonance on their not having encountered Jesus resurrected. But when they left Jerusalem prior to the end of the third day, they risked never seeing him at all ever again. That's because Jerusalem was where they might have expected Jesus to appear. But they left.

Danger

If the two disciples make it to Emmaus without encountering Jesus, they will miss out on their commission and participation in the mission Jesus had for them.

Emmaus story structure (using a Freytag Pyramid)

Exposition

Two disciples walk from Jerusalem to the village of Emmaus on the day of Jesus' resurrection. This day was part of the Feast of Unleavened Bread. The disciples talk with each other along the way about what had happened to Jesus and not seeing him resurrected.

Inciting Incident

Jesus draws near the two and begins walking with the disciples. He asks, "What is this conversation you are holding with each other as you walk?"

Rising Action

Stunned, the disciples feel a need to explain their profound disappointment in what happened to Jesus and in not seeing him resurrected. Jesus admonishes them and tells his story from the Scriptures. They ask Jesus to stay with them in Emmaus.

Climax

Jesus reveals himself to the disciples as he breaks bread with them.

I can only guess at what Jesus said when he blessed the bread and broke it and gave it to the two disciples. I know that the Feast of Unleavened Bread linked eating bread without leaven to more than one type of experience. The first was to the unpleasantness of suffering, established by association with bitter herbs (Ex. 12:8). The second was to rescue and redemption, tied to the day God brought Israel out of Egypt (Ex. 12:17). Given that leaven sometimes also represented corruption, it wouldn't surprise me to learn someday that the blessing Jesus gave was some combination of "This is my body..." (from the last supper, emphasizing suffering) and "For you will not abandon my soul to Sheol, or let your holy one see corruption" (from Psalm 16, emphasizing rescue and redemption as part of resurrection).

Falling Action

The disciples return to Jerusalem and tell the eleven what happened.

Resolution

Jesus appears to the two with the eleven as they gathered in the upper room.

Untying

Jesus commissions the two disciples and the eleven. Then Jesus ascends. Then the two and the eleven return to Jerusalem to wait for the Lord to clothe them with power from on high.

Answers to Emmaus Story Questions

Why were the two disciples heading to Emmaus, of all places?

The two disciples might have had mixed motives for heading to Emmaus. Emmaus could have been their hometown. But it also could have symbolized victory over political and religious corruption. See also below.

Why didn't they stay in Jerusalem beyond the morning of the third day?

Because the women who were first to the tomb in the morning of the third day didn't see Jesus. Their report seemed like an "idle tale."

Does Emmaus, as a location, hold any significance?

The story of how the village of Emmaus rose to prominence traces back to almost two hundred years before the story of the two disciples. Emmaus was where Antiochus Epiphanes chose many years before to station a contingent of soldiers to support a corrupt high priest. But things did not go well. His soldiers suffered defeat at the hand of Judah Maccabee, who had led a surprise attack against them. Maccabee led his men through the hills from Jerusalem to Emmaus to fight against the enemy. Following their victory, Emmaus took on a symbolic meaning. The simple lesson was this: *God delivers ordinary Jews from the power of corrupt kings and religious leaders.* This could be the reason for the two disciples choosing Emmaus as their destination. They were pursuing a renewed confidence in God's promises of deliverance.

It looks as though the two disciples travel from, and then back to, Jerusalem across the same hills as Judah Maccabee and his men. What a powerful image!

What is the significance of the distance between Emmaus and Jerusalem?

The distance was short enough to allow the two disciples to return to Jerusalem at once, even though it was night.

Why were the eyes of the two disciples kept from recognizing Jesus?

If the disciples had recognized Jesus right away, they may not have had the peak experience tied to hearing his story from the Scriptures. This underscores the value of hearing Jesus' story, even though we can't see Jesus. Hearing his story resolves dissonance.

Why did Luke name only one of the two disciples?

Nothing said in the text. Was one of the two a woman? It's also possible that no one knew the name of this person. Or perhaps that Luke had in mind a profound literary effect. Perhaps Luke intended for Theophilus and others to cast themselves in the role of the second disciple to help them through their own experiences of dissonance.

Was one of the two a woman?

Uncertain, but this adds another possibility to the previous answer.

Why did Jesus call the two disciples "fools and slow of heart"?

Because they did not connect the dots of Jesus' story themselves, even though they had been part of Jesus' inner circle.

Why did Jesus act like he was going on once they came near Emmaus?

Jesus was testing the disciples' response to his telling of his story. Perhaps the threat of his going on was a way of revealing to the disciples that their actual goal was not simply to get to Emmaus. Their actual goal was to resolve their dissonance. Since that tied to hearing the stranger's telling of Jesus' story, if the stranger left now, the power of their "new information" might fade. So, by threatening to go on, Jesus turned up the intensity of their actual desire.

Why did Jesus taking bread, blessing it, breaking it, and giving it to the two disciples lead to their eyes being opened?

The Feast of Unleavened Bread would have included a festive blessing over food. When Jesus gave his blessing, if he referred to the two purposes of the paschal lamb (redemption and restoration), the two disciples would have noticed. Perhaps all the more if his reference to redemption was the line he delivered at the last supper: "This is my body which was broken for you." And the second, a reference to his resurrection from Psalm 16: "For you will not abandon my soul to Sheol, or let your holy one see corruption." With Jesus' earlier telling of his larger story in mind, these things would have opened the disciples' eyes.

Why did Jesus vanish once the two disciples' eyes recognized him?

Because he wanted the two to return to Jerusalem to tell the eleven they had seen Jesus alive, not just in Jerusalem, but also in Emmaus.

What did the two disciples mean whey they said "Did not our hearts burn within us?"

A burning heart is a heart that's deeply moved and exhilarated. It is a response to a peak experience, one more aligned with consonance than dissonance. In the Emmaus story, the burning hearts of the disciples signal the end of their dissonance. The two disciples describe when this happened. It wasn't when Jesus revealed his identity. It was when Jesus told them his larger story from the Scriptures.

"Did not our *hearts burn within* us while he talked to us on the road, while he opened to us the Scriptures?" (Luke 24:32, emphasis mine)

Why was Jesus hungry?

Because he was in an actual physical body, a resurrected body, not a ghost.

Why did Jesus ask the disciples for food?

To show the disciples that he had raised from the dead bodily. He was not a ghost.

Why did Jesus lead the group out to Bethany in the end?

Bethany is the place where Jesus raised Lazarus from the dead and promised resurrection for everyone who believes in him.

How does the Emmaus story apply to life now?

We'll work on that next.

Story Deep

Chapter 12

Apply the Story

In this chapter, I'll craft a meaningful application of the Emmaus story. The application impacts how I tell or teach this story to others. But first, a word of caution.

Through the years, I've sat through many sermons on Bible stories, only to hear preachers shy away from telling what's there. I guess they are concerned people might not take an interest in the actual story. So they substitute some story of their own, or one they've heard or read.

For example, I once heard a preacher give a sermon about Peter, James, and John with Jesus on the mount of transfiguration. I believe this preacher was well meaning, but I also believe he lacked confidence in the actual story of Matthew 17. As if it wasn't enough. It seemed like he thought he had to prop it up with a story about his own experience hiking a tall mountain in Washington State (complete with slides). To this day, I don't understand why he did this. I believe he thought he was doing his audience a favor: Peter, James, and John with Jesus on a mountain somewhere? It won't be relevant, unless I can recall for people the time I hiked up Mt. Rainier with a few of my friends.

I believe every story told in Scripture can hold an audience without the help of a substitute story. Bible stories don't require us to prop them up. I believe they are relevant and engaging without us recounting something similar from our lives, or the lives of others. I also believe they suffer when we insist on substituting our own stories.

It so happens that I have some experience with hiking on mountains, including Mt. Rainier. Mt. Fuji too. In both cases, I didn't go all the way up. Still, I'm confident that none of my mountain treks parallel standing on the mount of transfiguration with Peter, James, and John experiencing Jesus' face shining like the sun and his clothes as white as light. It's the danger of substitute stories. They can rob audiences of opportunities to enter the lives and journeys of Bible characters; to experience the challenges they experienced on their journeys through life; and to grow from them.

I'm not saying we should never tell other stories. I'm saying that when we're preaching and teaching Bible stories, we need to give them a chance to do their work.

God designed Bible stories to engage our hearts and minds. They do this through their characters (with whom we share some bit of humanity); their characters' goals, and the motives that make their goals important; through the tension that rises from obstacles that block their way; and the risk and danger that decreases the likelihood of their characters' success; and through coherent sequences of events. Add in a meaningful core binary value and the empowerment of the Holy Spirit, and you have the formula for a compelling sermon or lesson.

The story of the two disciples on the road to Emmaus is a perfect example. Our story deep analysis of its core binary value, et al., shows that its lessons matter to our lives. We too can suffer from dissonance. Not just over questions about Jesus' death and resurrection. But also over pervasive rejections of our Christian worldview. We live, it seems, in a disconfirming biosphere; where politics, and the claims of science and false religion, all wreak their havoc.

Peter, who was there when the two returned from Emmaus to Jerusalem, refers to this modern type of disconfirmation in 2 Peter 3:

> "They will say, 'Where is the promise of his coming? For ever since
> the fathers fell asleep, all things are continuing as they were from
> the beginning of creation.'"

Peter indicates this worldview "overlooks" major elements of Jesus' larger story. He mentions the predictions of the holy prophets; the commandments of our Lord and Savior through the apostles; the creation account; the example of the Flood; the certainty of a day of judgment and destruction of the ungodly; and the promise of new heavens and a new earth. So the worldview Peter mentions is not just tied to the Flood as a historical event, but to several other components of the larger story as well. When the world denies these, dissonance threatens. But what's the solution?

Psychologists say that it could be doubling down on your existing beliefs. Or it could be acquiring new information. But what beliefs do we double down on? And what new information can we gain?

The Emmaus story gives the answer. The solution for any dissonance we experience today is the same as it was for the two disciples—learning more about Jesus and his larger story; and then doubling down. The solution is not seeing Jesus risen from the dead. If it were, we're sunk. We do not and cannot see Jesus today. But we can still listen to the larger story told about Jesus found in Scripture.

The two disciples heard Jesus' story twice. Once on the road to Emmaus. The second time when they were with the eleven. The structure of these tellings is similar in both cases. First there is dissonance/Jesus tells his story/Jesus reveals himself. Then there is Jesus reveals himself/Jesus tells his story/commissioning. In both cases, Jesus telling his story is central to what happens. This centrality stands out when you combine these structures and notice its chiastic form:

A. Dissonance

B. Jesus tells his story

C. Jesus reveals himself

C1. Jesus reveals himself

B1. Jesus tells his story

A1. Commissioning

This form shows emphasis on the middle statements; Jesus reveals himself. But it also shows emphasis on Jesus tells his story. In the first instance, Jesus tells his story and then reveals himself. In the second, he reveals himself and then tells his story. The reversal adds to our understanding of just how central Jesus telling his story is. The first time provides context for Jesus revealing himself. The second provides warrant for his commissioning.

In the end, all the emphasis on Jesus' larger story in Scripture underscores the central role it plays in our lives, too. We are to know it and rehearse it. Like the two disciples, we are also to use it to resolve the dissonance we experience in the world, and make sense of our own commission to serve with Jesus' blessing and empowerment.

But modern biases interfere with our engaging Jesus' story as story. They lead us instead to treat Jesus' story as more of a theological treatise. We dissect and systematize. We end up telling more of a director's cut than a story. Not that this is all bad. It's not. Still, we never quite grasp the whole. So instead of the consonance that comes from a story-first approach, the consequence for many is faith-diminishing, sometimes even faith-destroying, dissonance.

Could this be a reason why so many churches are in decline? And why so many Millennials and Generations Zs are turning away? Why they're looking elsewhere for community, sacred space, and peak experiences? Even a casual review of the research shows these trends. In the end, the solution to these and other dissonance-related problems is the same as the solution for the disciples on the Road to Emmaus; a restored confidence in the larger story of Jesus; and in the power of a story-first approach.

Chapter 13

Teach the Story

In this chapter, I'm going to offer some guidance on how to preach or teach the Emmaus the story. To be honest, this has been the most difficult chapter for me to write. For one, there is more than one way to preach or teach through this story. For two, factors beyond my explanations in this book influence the way I would preach or teach through this story. I hope to share more about preaching and teaching, and telling Bible stories in a future work. For three, every preaching or teaching situation differs from every other. I usually teach and preach to adults. You might teach teens, or even children. These differences mean you, as the reader, will have to take what I offer and adapt it to your situation.

Here's an example of how I would preach or teach this story:

First, I would read aloud the text, beginning with Luke 24:13 and ending for now with verse 35. Next, I would pray and ask the Lord to guide our study of his Word. Then I would introduce the story:

Today, I'm going to walk you through the details of a familiar Bible story about two of Jesus' disciples; two disciples who were confused by what the world threw at them, much like what happens to you and me. And I think you're going to find this interesting, because these two discovered how to sort through their confusion and renew their dedication in service to our Lord. Here's what happened...

Notice I am NOT beginning with a substitute story. I'm beginning with a tease about the actual story. My tease uses what's called the X/Y formula:

I'm going to tell you a story about X, and I think you'll find it interesting because of Y.

The X/Y formula allows me to identify the main characters (the two disciples); their inward goal (overcome their confusion over what the world threw at them), and the story's untying (renew their dedication in service to the Lord). By saying, "much like what happens to you and me," I have invited my audience into empathizing with the main characters. I have signaled to them that the story is as much about them as it is about the main characters.

From here, I would take one of two paths (it's the Emmaus story, but no pun intended). I would either retell the story, casting my audience in the role of the unnamed disciple (see Appendix B), or I would go through the story and explain what happened beat by beat. Remember, a story beat is a unit of action/reaction.

Here's how the latter approach may work:

Our story begins with two disciples, one of them named, one of them not, walking from Jerusalem for about 7 miles to a village named Emmaus. We'll find out in a few minutes Emmaus was not just any village. It held some very special significance in the hearts and minds of our two disciples.

Now keep in mind, these disciples were followers of Jesus. They believed Jesus was a mighty prophet, sent by God; that he was the one, they hoped, who was to redeem Israel.

But then they saw what the chief priests and rulers had done to Jesus. They had delivered Jesus to be condemned to death and cruci-fied. We don't know this for sure, but it seems they must have seen Jesus suffer and die on the cross.

And today is the third day, the day Jesus had said he would rise again.

Sure enough, some women from the group visited Jesus' tomb early that morning. And it was empty. The women said they saw angels there, and the angels said that Jesus was alive. So some of the men went to check it out. The tomb was empty alright, but they did NOT see Jesus.

Notice I am using material from the story itself as exposition.

Can you imagine the confusion and disappointment as these things swirled through the minds of the two disciples? They could remem-ber Jesus' teachings and the mighty deeds he performed. But now, none of it seemed to line up. And they felt profound discomfort over this. Psychologists call this discomfort cognitive dissonance. Or just dissonance. People experience dissonance when their be-liefs, or even things they know, don't line up. Or worse yet, when they contradict each other.

When something important is at stake, people will feel pressure to relieve their discomfort. They may change their beliefs. They may seek new information. Or they may just turn away altogether from any reminders of their dissonance.

In our story, the two disciples left Jerusalem and head for Emmaus.

Now you may wonder, is there any significance to Emmaus as their destination? And the answer is, Possibly.

This is where I will bring in some of the background information I uncovered about the village of Emmaus and its history. I'm doing this to answer a story question I believe my audience could ask themselves. "Is there any significance to Emmaus as the disciples' destination?"

Nearly two hundred years before, there was a corrupt high priest ruling in Jerusalem. He was weak enough that he could not hold power without help. So Antiochus Epiphanes sent his army to nearby Emmaus to project power to support the high priest. But things did not go well. Ordinary Jews hated them. One night, Judah Maccabee led a group of men through the hills from Jerusalem to Emmaus to launch a surprise attack. Maccabee and his rag-tag volunteers routed Antiochus' soldiers. Following their victory, Emmaus took on a symbolic meaning. The simple lesson was this. God delivers ordinary Jews from the power of corrupt kings and religious leaders. This could be the reason for the two disciples choosing Emmaus as their destination. They were pursuing a renewed confidence in God's promises of deliverance. And so they headed for a village that symbolized that.

Notice I'm saying this could be the significance of Emmaus as the destination of the two disciples.

Despite what the two disciples thought that Emmaus could do for them, they could not clear their minds of what happened. They had to talk about it.

But then Jesus himself drew near and started walking with them. However, "their eyes were kept from recognizing him." That's an interesting way to put that. Not, "they didn't recognize him." But, "their eyes were kept from recognizing him." I think it foreshadows a purpose Jesus had in mind for not allowing them to recognize him. We'll find out what that purpose is as we keep going.

Now I can imagine the two disciples NOT wanting to talk to a stranger about their dissonance. I can imagine them being embarrassed for their mistaken beliefs about Jesus. "How could we be so wrong?"

But, as I say, Jesus had a purpose for joining the two disciples on their walk. So you know he will not let them keep to themselves. Sure enough, he asks, "What is this conversation that you are holding with each other as you walk?"

Isn't this just like Jesus? Just kind of easing his way in. Not confronting them. Not saying, "What are you two doing leaving Jerusalem? Are you going to give up that easily?"

But one of the two disciples doesn't respond with such grace. He insults Jesus. "Are you the only visitor to Jerusalem who does not know the things that have happened there in these days?

Insulting Jesus. Isn't that just like us, too?

Jesus brushes aside the insult and asks, "What things?"

The two disciples explain their disappointment and confusion in detail. Let's take another look at what they said, beginning in verse 19:

And they said to him, "Concerning Jesus of Nazareth, a man who was a prophet mighty in deed and word before God and all the people, [20] and how our chief priests and rulers delivered him up to be condemned to death, and crucified him. [21] But we had hoped that he was the one to redeem Israel. Yes, and besides all this, it is now the third day since these things happened. [22] Moreover, some women of our company amazed us. They were at the tomb early in the morning, [23] and when they did not find his body, they came back saying that they had even seen a vision of angels, who said that he was alive. [24] Some of those who were with us went to the tomb and found it just as the women had said, but him they did not see."

It sure seems like their feelings of disappointment and confusion were right there. Just below the surface, and ready to erupt. It also seems like they were portraying themselves as very rational. That they had good reasons to feel disappointed and confused. As though they were saying to Jesus, "You understand, don't you?"

But Jesus would not coddle them. In fact, he insults them. "O foolish ones," he said, "and slow of heart to believe all that the prophets have spoken! Was it not necessary that the Christ should suffer these things and enter into his glory?"

It was an insult, but not a punishing one. Jesus meant to shock the two disciples into listening to every word he would say next. "And beginning with Moses and all the Prophets, he interpreted to them in all the Scriptures the things concerning himself."

Notice that I will continue telling the story from here. I won't insert what I know about the "burning hearts" of the two disciples just yet.

Eventually, Jesus and the two disciples draw near to Emmaus. Jesus "acts" like he's going to continue on. Why did he do that? I'm not sure. But from a story perspective, the possibility of Jesus going on without revealing himself creates tension in us. It makes us want to break into the story to tell the disciples, "Don't let him go! There's something about this stranger you don't know yet!"

Well, as things play out, the two disciples don't let Jesus go. They urge him to stay, but they're not honest about the reason. They tell Jesus it's because the day is almost over. But it's likely that the real reason is they wanted to hear more.

So Jesus stays with the two disciples and shares a meal with them. Here's what Luke says: "When Jesus was at table with them, he took the bread and blessed and broke it and gave it to them. And their eyes were opened, and they recognized him. And he vanished from their sight."

The question, of course, is what about Jesus taking the bread and blessing it, and then breaking it and giving it to the two disciples opened their eyes? What made them recognize Jesus?

I believe we find the answer in remembering the timing of this meal shared between Jesus and the two disciples. It's still Sunday. The Passover was Friday. That means our story falls within the time frame of the Feast of Unleavened Bread.

Many Jewish rabbis find two themes in what the book of Exodus chapter 12 has to say about the Feast of Unleavened Bread. Both have something to do with Passover. The first is suffering. The second is redemption and restoration. Exodus 12:8 connects eating unleavened bread with eating bitter herbs during the Passover meal. That represents suffering. Then Exodus 12:17 adds: "And you shall observe the Feast of Unleavened Bread, for on this very day I brought your hosts out of the land of Egypt." That's redemption and restoration.

Back to our story. What if Jesus referred to the two themes as he blessed and broke the bread and gave it to the two disciples? If he did, the two disciples would have noticed. Especially if his reference to suffering in the blessing was identical to what he said at the last supper: "This is my body which was broken for you." Jesus could have followed with a reference to his resurrection in the second part of his blessing. Keep in mind, Jesus' resurrection was a witness to God's promise of restoration. And it was proof of the redemption that is through the shedding of Jesus' blood. What if Jesus quoted from Psalm 16:10 in the last part of his blessing: "For you will not abandon my soul to Sheol, or let your holy one see corruption"?

I admit I'm speculating. Whatever Jesus said, it was enough to clue in the two disciples.

Then Jesus vanished from their sight. Why? Because this story is not about Jesus lingering with the two disciples. He has something in mind for them to do.

But first the two disciples talk with each other about what happened. This is where in the story we find them saying: "Did not our hearts burn within us while he talked to us on the road, while he opened to us the Scriptures?"

Now the story goes on from here. The two disciples return to Jerusalem. They meet up with the eleven. Then Jesus appears to them all. Only this time, Jesus reveals himself right away, telling his beloved disciples: "See my hands and my feet, that it is I myself." Afterwards, Jesus ate with them. Then, for a second time, Jesus reached into the Law of Moses, the Prophets, and the Psalms to tell his story. Then he commissioned them to proclaim the gospel in his name to all nations, promising to empower them with power from on high.

But I want to go back to what the two disciples said about their "hearts burning within them." These words point to the disciples having what's called a peak experience. Peak experiences are not common experiences. They are unique and deeply moving. And they exhilarate you.

This exhilaration of the two disciples signals their return to consonance. No longer are they suffering from dissonance. Now they can make sense of things.

Notice what led to the change. It wasn't the opening of their eyes to recognize Jesus, though I'm sure that was a blessing. The two disciples say their hearts started burning within them BEFORE their eyes were opened to recognize Jesus. So what set their hearts on fire? It was hearing Jesus tell his larger story from Scripture. Jesus connected the dots for them, and it made sense. And it thrilled them to the core.

Now that I've told the story of the two disciples, it's time to make application.

When I started today, I said: "I'm going to walk you through the details of a familiar Bible story about two of Jesus' disciples, who were confused by what the world threw at them." And I said that's "much like what happens to you and me."

It's so true. The world throws something at us that leaves us disappointed and confused. It could be an experience of loss. Or a matter of public opinion that stands contrary to everything we believe. It could be a claim of an expert, a scientist even, that appears to prove our Christian worldview isn't accurate. Or just the march of a secular culture farther and farther away from God and Jesus-centered values. It could be the delay of Christ's return. Or the apparent triumph of evil over good. Whatever it is, it can lead to experiences of dissonance.

Here's the thing. If the dissonance is severe enough, like the two disciples, we also will feel pressure to relieve our discomfort. Some seek new information. Some give in and change their beliefs. Some turn away altogether.

So what's the solution?

One thing we know. The solution is NOT Jesus appearing to us and proving that he rose from the dead. That will be great when it finally happens. Meanwhile, if that's the only solution, we're sunk. We do not and cannot see Jesus today.

In the end, the solution is the same for us as it was for the two disciples—learning more about Jesus and his larger story; and then doubling down. Like the two disciples, we can hear the larger story told in Scripture about Jesus. The two disciples heard Jesus' story twice. Once on the road to Emmaus. The second time when they were with the eleven. The first time Jesus tells his story and then reveals himself. In the second, he reveals himself and then tells his story. This reversal shows how central Jesus telling his story is. It provides context for Jesus revealing himself in the first instance. In the second, it provides warrant for his commissioning.

Now I have to say, I'm especially concerned for the Millennials, the Gen Z, and the Nones among us. Modern biases interfere with our engaging Jesus' story as *story*. They lead us instead to treat Jesus' story as more of a theological treatise. We dissect and systematize. We end up telling more of a director's cut than a story. Not that this is all bad. It's not. Still, we never quite grasp the whole. So instead of the consonance that comes from a story-first approach, the consequence for many is faith-diminishing, sometimes even faith-destroying, dissonance.

Could this be why so many churches are in decline? And why so many Millennials, Gen Z's, and Nones are turning away? Why they're looking elsewhere for community and sacred space? And for peak experiences? Even a casual review of the research shows these trends.

Our story's emphasis on Jesus' larger story in Scripture underscores the role it plays in our lives too. We are to know it and rehearse it.

Story Deep

Like the two disciples, we are also to use it to resolve any dissonance we experience in the world, and to make sense of our own commission to serve with Jesus' blessing and empowerment.

Leveling Up the Application

As I finish telling the Emmaus story, I will ask people to do three things. First, to believe in Jesus, if they have not already done so. I will also acknowledge that someone might desire to hear more about Jesus before they believe. So I will also offer to share more of Jesus' story at another time, including the reasons why he had to suffer and die on the cross. When the time comes, I will share a summary of Jesus' larger story similar to the one I wrote in Chapter 5.

The second thing I will ask Christians to do is reacquaint themselves with Jesus' larger story in Scripture. Read it, study it, and don't stop until it makes sense as a story. Too many Christians, and even many Bible teachers, don't even try to make story sense of major sections of the Scriptures. Ask yourself, for example, where do the stories of the Flood in Genesis 6 and of the Tower of Babel Story in Genesis 11 fit in Jesus' larger story? What do they have to do with Jesus? What do they have to do with the New Testament or the book of Revelation in particular?

Third, I will ask listeners to join me in teaching Jesus' larger story to the next generation. According to research, a larger percentage of Generation Z is open to hearing more about Jesus. We need parents, children's ministry workers, and student ministry leaders to double down on making Jesus' story known. By the way, sharing Jesus' larger story with others requires you to reacquaint with it first and then to practice telling it in a way that makes story sense. Repeating it to yourself and others will not only pass it on to the next generation. It will also grow your familiarity with it, and your heart-deep appreciation for Jesus. You might even join me in making the same promise I included at the beginning of the book: to use Jesus' story to better tell who he is; to foster appreciative love for him; to connect the dots of Scripture and communicate the connections, to practice a Jesus-centered worldview; and to prepare myself and others for Jesus' return.

Fourth, I will also ask listeners to find additional practical ways of letting Jesus' larger story impact their lives and service for Christ. The world full of counter-stories, all of them capable of ginning up dissonance and making us question the sanity of our love for Jesus. To endure, we must double-down on Jesus' larger story. It's the most powerful strategy of all.

Appendix A

The Story Deep Process At a Glance

Read the Story

Do this several times to become familiar with the story.

Ask Story Questions

Look for questions that arise from your readings of the story. Answers to these questions are required to make sense of what happens in the story. For example, in the Emmaus story, *Why were the two disciples kept from recognizing Jesus?*

Take Notice of Story Elements

Story elements include such things as main character, goal, motive, etc. They also include techniques that storytellers use in their craft.

Check the Larger Story

This involves finding out where and how a particular story fits into the larger overarching narrative of Scripture.

Look At Other Material from the Same Author

This helps to determine where a particular story begins and ends, along with where and how it fits within the theme(s) of writing from the same author.

Create a Step Outline

The purpose of this type of outline is to state what happens in a story one action at a time. An action could be something a character does or says.

Treat the Step Outline

This process calls attention to the subtext beneath the actions listed in the step outline.

Treat the Story's Structure

Use this step to fill in the elements of story structure with the observations and classifications you've made in the previous two steps. This is also where you will make sense of the action/reaction patterns you observe in the story.

Summarize and Answer Story Questions

Circle back to the story questions you asked at the beginning and summarize answers.

Apply and Teach the Story

Pass on to others the treasures of meaning you've uncovered in your study.

Getting Started

The *story deep* process may seem overwhelming at first. But I assure you, in time you will grow comfortable with it And you will become more proficient in using it. Meanwhile, practice is the key.

- Practice your awareness of story elements. For example, identify the story's main character, his or her goal, and motive; and the story's core binary value.

- Practice looking for sequences of action/reaction among the characters in the story, keeping in mind that dialogue is a kind of action.

- Practice looking for when sequences of action/reaction change the charge of a story's core binary value.

- Practice analyzing where and how the story fits into the larger story told in Scripture, along with where and how the story fits into other writings from the same author.

Once you've practice these, you'll be well on your way to following the rest of the *story deep* process. You'll also become more comfortable with starting from the beginning and working your way through each step.

Appendix B

Gospel Story-arc Apologetics

The Unnamed Disciple On the Road to Emmaus

E veryone knows that Luke names only one of the two disciples who encountered Jesus on the road to Emmaus. Why is that?

Is it because the unnamed disciple is a woman? Did he or she ask to be left unnamed? What if the person who told Luke this story just couldn't remember the name?

Or what if Luke knew that leaving the second disciple unnamed would provoke a profound literary effect? One that might prompt Theophilus, his target audience, or any other reader, to cast themselves in that role?

Which leads me to ask, what if the unnamed disciple is you?

Imagine the confusion, the disappointment, the weight of each step, as you trudge the seven miles or so from Jerusalem to Emmaus, alongside Cleopas, the other disciple.

"How much farther?" you ask out loud.

But the only reply you hear has nothing to do with the road in front of you. It is the sound instead of a deep sigh, a breath of despair, expelled from your chest, as though it could be your last.

Jesus is dead, you repeat to yourself. The Christ and Redeemer of Israel is dead. By crucifixion no less, and with the blessing of Israel's rulers and priests, men who should have known better.

And therein lies the problem, because now you know better too, as the voice in your head keeps reminding you:

How could I have been so wrong? So gullible?

If Jesus were the Christ, he shouldn't have died. And if he did die, he shouldn't have stayed dead.

I will never play the fool again.

And that goes too for all the talk about angels dressed in dazzling apparel, standing outside Jesus' tomb, and telling the women he had risen from the dead.

But Jesus wasn't there, was he.

Suddenly you realize there's only one way to stop shaming yourself. You must let go of the hope that clouded your judgment and throw down your deepest beliefs about Jesus. You must return instead to the life you once knew.

That means going back to Emmaus.

You call to mind the famous battle of Emmaus from two hundred years earlier. The Seleucid leader, Antiochus IV, had ordered soldiers under the command of Apollonius to encamp at Emmaus, because of its proximity to Jerusalem. The soldiers' mission was to enforce the authority of the puppet high priest that Antiochus had installed in Jerusalem.

Antiochus' support of Israel's corrupt religious establishment gave rise to the still famous revolt of the Maccabees. One night, Judah Maccabee and his ragtag volunteers stole through the hills outside of Jerusalem to launch an early morning surprise attack against the encampment at Emmaus. Though the Seleucid soldiers were greater in number, better trained, and better equipped, the Maccabees defeated them soundly.

Judah Maccabee's triumph over Apollonius at Emmaus became no less symbolic than the victory of America's George Washington over Hessian soldiers at the Battle of Trenton in 1776. Like Judah Maccabee, George Washington led a group of ragtag soldiers on a nighttime march in a surprise attack against a superior force. But unlike the notoriety given Washington's route via the Delaware River, in the case of Judah Maccabee, the fame fell to the battlefield.

And so you traipse on, recalling the glory of Emmaus, imagining what it's like for ordinary Jews like you to triumph over tyrants, even if it didn't work out this time.

As you and Cleopas occupy yourselves with laments of disappointment in Jesus, a mysterious stranger approaches. He overhears you talking and asks, "What is this conversation that you are holding with each other as you walk?"

You pause. Not even the glory of former victories in Emmaus can stop the flood of emotions lurking just below the surface. Your heart races.

Doesn't he see the vacant look on my face? The redness of my eyes? The slump of my shoulders?

You bend to a crouching position. You want to answer the stranger, but you have no words. The kind of dissonance you're experiencing never resolves itself easily.

Finally, Cleopas breaks the silence: "Are you the only visitor to Jerusalem who does not know the things that have happened there in these days?"

The stranger says, "What things?"

You stand now to join Cleopas, though you position yourself slightly behind him. The two of you take turns filling in: "Concerning Jesus of Nazareth, a man who was a prophet mighty in deed and word before God and all the people, and how our chief priests and rulers delivered him up to be condemned to death, and crucified him. But we had hoped that he was the one to redeem Israel. Yes, and besides all this, it is now the third day since these things happened. Moreover, some women of our company amazed us. They were at the tomb early in the morning, and when they did not find his body, they came back saying that they had even seen a vision of angels, who said that he was alive. Some of those who were with us went to the tomb and found it just as the women had said, but him they did not see."

So there it is, you say to yourself, as you lower your eyes. That's what we believed about Jesus and why we're so disappointed. Surely you understand.

But then the stranger says: "O foolish ones, and slow of heart to believe all that the prophets have spoken! Was it not necessary that the Christ should suffer these things and enter into his glory?"

The stranger's words echo in your mind: He called me a fool. And slow of heart. Has he no sympathy? I wasted three years of my life and have nothing to show for it.

In the split second that follows, your mind turns to the question the stranger asked: "Was it not necessary that the Christ should suffer these things and enter into his glory?"

Before you or Cleopas can respond, the stranger starts sharing the larger story of the Christ, "beginning with Moses and all the Prophets," and continuing on "through all the Scriptures."

A deep and intense feeling grips your heart, as you listen to the stranger's story. But you're almost to Emmaus, and you need to stop for the night.

When you arrive, the stranger acts as though he will walk on. So you urge him to stay, hoping he will share more.

He agrees.

It is the evening of the second full day of the Feast of Unleavened Bread. You and Cleopas and the stranger sit together for a meal. You watch as the stranger takes the bread and blesses it. Then he breaks it and gives it to you and to Cleopas.

But wait, you say to yourself, the blessing he just gave...

I bless Yahweh who gives me counsel;
in the night also my heart instructs me.

I have set Yahweh always before me;
because he is at my right hand, I shall not be shaken.

Therefore my heart is glad, and my whole being rejoices;
my flesh also dwells secure.

For you will not abandon my soul to Sheol,
or let your holy one see corruption.

Why those are words of David from Psalm 16.

And he finished with Jesus' words from the night he was betrayed: "This is my body, which is given for you. Do this in remembrance of me."

Immediately your eyes are open. The eyes of Cleopas too. Both of you recognize the stranger is no stranger at all.

"It's Jesus!" You exclaim.

Then he disappears.

When you turn back to Cleopas, you see on his face a look of indescribable joy. Both of you cry out at once: "Did not our hearts burn within us while he talked to us on the road, while he opened to us the Scriptures?"

You realize that your feelings of disappointment and shame have vanished. In their place, you sense something so profound, so intense, so overpowering—your heart feels more alive now than ever before.

It's late and the road is dark. But you and Cleopas cannot wait. Like Judah Maccabee of old, you scamper through the hills near Emmaus at night, but this time toward Jerusalem, and not to launch a surprise attack, but to share the good news: "Jesus walked with us on the road and broke bread with us. He's alive!"

Epilogue

Jesus appears for a second time to Cleopas and the unnamed disciple after they returned to Jerusalem and gathered with the eleven. Only this time, Jesus reveals himself right away, telling his beloved disciples: "See my hands and my feet, that it is I myself." Afterwards Jesus ate with them. Then, as before, Jesus reached into the Law of Moses, the Prophets, and the Psalms to tell his story a second time. Finally, he commissioned them to proclaim the gospel in his name to all nations, promising to empower them with power from on high.

Appendix C

Gospel Story-arc Apologetics

A Story-first Approach

If I had to select only one Bible story to represent the apologetics tied to the Gospel Story-arc® Project, I would choose Luke's account of the two disciples on the road to Emmaus. Their experiences with Jesus show the transforming power of a story-first approach. It's the kind of power we need now so desperately. Like the disciples on the road to Emmaus, we too suffer from a kind of dissonance. Not just over questions about Jesus' death and resurrection. But also over pervasive rejections of our Christian worldview. We live, it seems, in a disconfirming biosphere; where politics, and the claims of science and false religion, all wreak their havoc.

Peter, who was there when the two returned from Emmaus to Jerusalem, refers to this modern type of disconfirmation in 2 Peter 3:

> They will say, "Where is the promise of his coming? For ever since the fathers fell asleep, all things are continuing as they were from the beginning of creation."

Peter indicates this worldview "overlooks" major elements of Jesus' larger story. He mentions the predictions of the holy prophets; the commandments of our Lord and Savior through the apostles; the creation account; the example of the

Flood; the certainty of a day of judgment and destruction of the ungodly; and the promise of new heavens and a new earth. So the worldview Peter mentions is not just tied to the Flood as a historical event, but to several other components of the larger story as well. When the world denies these, dissonance threatens. But what's the solution?

Psychologists say that it could be doubling down on your existing beliefs. Or it could be acquiring new information. But what beliefs do we double down on? And what new information can we gain?

The Emmaus story gives the answer. The solution for any dissonance we experience today is the same as it was for the two disciples—learning more about Jesus and his larger story; and then doubling down. The solution is not seeing Jesus risen from the dead. If it were, we're sunk. We do not and cannot see Jesus today. But we can still listen to the larger story told about Jesus found in Scripture.

The two disciples heard Jesus' story twice. Once on the road to Emmaus. The second time when they were with the eleven. The structure of these tellings is similar in both cases. First there is dissonance/Jesus tells his story/Jesus reveals himself. Then there is Jesus reveals himself/Jesus tells his story/commissioning. In both cases, Jesus telling his story is central to what happens. This centrality stands out when you combine these structures and notice its chiastic form:

A. Dissonance

B. Jesus tells his story

C. Jesus reveals himself

C1. Jesus reveals himself

B1. Jesus tells his story

A1. Commissioning

This form shows emphasis on the middle statements; Jesus reveals himself. But is also shows emphasis on Jesus tells his story. In the first instance, Jesus tells his story and then reveals himself. In the second, he reveals himself and then tells his story. The reversal adds to our understanding of just how central Jesus telling his story is. The first time provides context for Jesus revealing himself. The second provides warrant for his commissioning.

In the end, all the emphasis on Jesus' larger story in Scripture underscores the role it plays in our lives, too. We are to know it and rehearse it. Like the two disciples, we are also to use it to resolve the dissonance we experience in the world, and make sense of our own commission to serve with Jesus' blessing and empowerment.

But modern biases interfere with our engaging Jesus' story as story. They lead us instead to treat Jesus' story as more of a theological treatise. We dissect and systematize. We end up telling more of a director's cut than a story. Not that this is all bad. It's not. Still, we never quite grasp the whole. So instead of the consonance that comes from a story-first approach, the consequence for many is faith-diminishing, sometimes even faith-destroying, dissonance.

Could this be a reason why so many churches are in decline? And why so many Millennials and Generations Zs are turning away? Why they're looking elsewhere for community and sacred space? And for peak experiences? Even a casual review of the research shows these trends. In the end, the solution to these and other dissonance-related problems is the same as the solution for the disciples on the Road to Emmaus—a restored confidence in the larger story of Jesus and in the power of a story-first approach.

For more from the Gospel Story-arc Project, go to https://gospelstoryarc.org.

A Final Word

The tagline for the Gospel Story-arc Project is *It's Your Story Too!* Perhaps you remember seeing these words beneath the GSA logo at the front of this book. Sometimes when people hear our tagline, they think it's just a trendy way of telling them to get on board with telling their own life story. But the story in our tagline is not our personal story; it's Jesus' story.

When we use a Freytag pyramid to represent the structure of the Bible's larger story about Jesus, we can see that we are living now in the story's falling action. The climax of Jesus' story ends with his ascension to the right hand of the Father. The resolution begins with Jesus' return. In between is the falling action. In this sense, Jesus' story is our story too. To make it more personal, *It's Your Story Too!*

Knowing that we're living within Jesus' story helps us to keep our heads in times of trouble. It invites us to interpret things happening around us in ways that line up with the coming resolution and untying. As the time of Jesus' return nears, this way of looking at life and our place in the world will become increasingly more important. Just as it did at other times in history when it seemed as though Jesus' story was no longer in play.

I pray that *Story Deep* will motivate you to reacquaint yourself with the Bible's larger story about Jesus as an all-encompassing worldview. And that you will join me in honoring Jesus for who he truly is, the Christ, the Son of God, and Lord of lords.

Story Deep

To learn more about the power of story and story hermeneutics, take advantage of GSA resources available at http://gospelstoryarc.org. Or if I can serve you in some other way, please reach out to me on social media. And help us spread the word.

It's Your Story Too!

—Randal Gilmore

Find more Story Deep resources here:

About the Author

Randal Gilmore (Doctor of Religious Studies, Trinity Seminary, Newburgh, IN) is the Founder and Director of The Gospel Story-arc Project, a ministry initiative that uses the science of story to aid in Bible exposition and better tell who Jesus is.He is a longtime pastor and missions leader, having most recently served as the Regional Director for WOL ministries in the Indo-Pacific Region. He is the author of numerous books, including **The Sparrow and the Tortoise** (Exalt Publications) and **Exalted Lord** (Exalt Publications). He is also a contributing author of **The Pastor** (RBP).

Other Books by Randal Gilmore

The Sparrow and the Tortoise

Jesus' First Miracle

Exalted Lord

How to Find Agreement in a Disagreeable World

Made in the USA
Columbia, SC
30 March 2023

df86d0be-fdea-44b3-99ac-593c2487fdeaR01